# **S**uper **R**eview™

*All You Need to Know!*

# PSYCHOLOGY II

**By the Staff of
Research & Education Association
Dr. M. Fogiel, Director**

*Research & Education Association*
61 Ethel Road West
Piscataway, New Jersey 08854

# SUPER REVIEW™
# OF PSYCHOLOGY II

Printed in the United States of America

Library of Congress Catalog Card Number 00-133919

International Standard Book Number 0-87891-090-5

SUPER REVIEW is a trademark of
Research & Education Association, Piscataway, New Jersey 08854

# REA's Books Are The Best...
## They have rescued lots of grades and more!

(a sample of the <u>hundreds of letters</u> REA receives each year)

"Your books are great! They are very helpful, and have upped my grade in every class. Thank you for such a great product."
*Student, Seattle, WA*

"Your book has really helped me sharpen my skills and improve my weak areas. Definitely will buy more."
*Student, Buffalo, NY*

"Compared to the other books that my fellow students had, your book was the most useful in helping me get a great score."
*Student, North Hollywood, CA*

"I really appreciate the help from your excellent book. Please keep up your great work."
*Student, Albuquerque, NM*

"Your book was such a better value and was so much more complete than anything your competition has produced (and I have them all)!"
*Teacher, Virginia Beach, VA*

*(more on next page)*

*(continued from previous page)*

"Your books have saved my GPA, and quite possibly my sanity. My course grade is now an 'A', and I couldn't be happier."

*Student, Winchester, IN*

"These books are the best review books on the market. They are fantastic!"

*Student, New Orleans, LA*

"Your book was responsible for my success on the exam. . . I will look for REA the next time I need help."

*Student, Chesterfield, MO*

"I think it is the greatest study guide I have ever used!"

*Student, Anchorage, AK*

"I encourage others to buy REA because of their superiority. Please continue to produce the best quality books on the market."

*Student, San Jose, CA*

"Just a short note to say thanks for the great support your book gave me in helping me pass the test . . . I'm on my way to a B.S. degree because of you !"

*Student, Orlando, FL*

# WHAT THIS Super Review WILL DO FOR YOU

This **Super Review** provides all that you need to know to do your homework effectively and succeed on exams and quizzes.

The book focuses on the core aspects of the subject, and helps you to grasp the important elements quickly and easily.

Outstanding **Super Review** features:

- Topics are covered in logical sequence

- Topics are reviewed in a concise and comprehensive manner

- The material is presented in student-friendly language that makes it easy to follow and understand

- Individual topics can be easily located

- Provides excellent preparation for midterms, finals and in-between quizzes

- In every chapter, reviews of individual topics are accompanied by Questions **Q** and Answers **A** that show how to work out specific problems

- At the end of most chapters, quizzes with answers are included to enable you to practice and test yourself to pinpoint your strengths and weaknesses

- Written by professionals and test experts who function as your very own tutors

Dr. Max Fogiel
Program Director

# CONTENTS

# 7 SOCIAL BEHAVIOR

# CHAPTER 1

# Human Development

## 1.1 Physical and Perceptual Development

**Developmental psychologists** study age-related changes that occur throughout the life span, from conception until death. Traditionally, developmental psychologists have focused on childhood, but other periods of development are studied as well.

The **nature vs. nurture** debate has motivated the study of development. That is, is a person's development determined by **heredity** or by **environment**? Psychologists today recognize that both nature and nurture interact to influence the developmental process.

**Heredity** is the transmission of ancestral characteristics from parents to offspring through the genes. **Genes** determine hereditary characteristics and are the chemical blueprints of all living things. Genes are made up of **DNA** or **deoxyribonucleic acid** and possess the information that determines the makeup of every cell in our body. Genes lie along **chromosomes,** bodies that are in the nucleus of each cell in our body. Every human body cell (except the sex cells) contains **46** chromosomes arranged in **23 pairs**.

The **sex cells** (**ova** or egg cell in the female and **sperm** in the male) contain **23 single** chromosomes. Fertilization results in **23 pairs** of chromosomes – one member of each pair is contributed by the mother, the other by the father.

Every female egg contains an **X chromosome** and every male sperm cell contains *either* an **X** or a **Y chromosome**. At conception, if the egg is fertilized by a sperm carrying a Y chromosome, the offspring will be **XY** or male. If the egg is fertilized by a sperm carrying an X chromosome, the child will be **XX** or female.

**Genotype** is a term used to refer to an individual's genetic make-up.

**Phenotype** refers to how a given genotype is expressed (i.e., what the person looks like or how the person behaves). Phenotype occurs as a result of an interaction between genotype and environment.

**Dominant genes** are expressed in an individual's phenotype whenever they are present in the genotype. **Recessive genes** are expressed in an individual's phenotype only when they are paired with a similar recessive gene.

### 1.1.1 Prenatal Development

**Prenatal** development refers to the period of development from conception to birth. The average pregnancy lasts 270 days or 40 weeks.

At conception, the **female egg** or **ovum** is fertilized by the **male sperm**, usually in the **Fallopian tube**. This results in a **fertilized egg** that is called a **zygote**. The zygote repeatedly divides as it travels down the Fallopian tube to the **uterus**, where it becomes attached to the uterine wall.

The three stages of prenatal development are outlined below:

**Ovum** or **Germinal**  The first two weeks after conception. Is a microscopic mass of multiplying cells. Zygote travels down Fallopian tube and implants itself on the wall of the uterus. **Placenta** (provides nourishment and allows wastes to pass out to the mother) begins to form. **Umbilical cord** carries nourishment from and waste to the placenta. Thin membranes keep fetal and maternal bloodstreams separate.

**Embryonic**          Second to eighth week after conception. Only about one inch long by end of this stage. Most vital organs and bodily systems *begin* to form. Major birth defects are often due to problems that occur during this stage. An **amniotic sac**, or fluid-filled sac, surrounds the embryo to serve as protection and provide a constant temperature.

**Fetal**              From two months after conception until birth. Muscles and bones form. Vital organs continue to grow and begin to function. During last three months, brain develops rapidly.

## Problem Solving Examples:

 List and define the three major periods of prenatal development.

 The first major period of gestation (the time between conception and birth) is the preimplantation period. This period lasts about two weeks during which time the zygote (previously called the fertilized ovum) moves down the Fallopian tube and implants itself in the wall of the uterus.

The second period is that of the embryo. This period lasts until the eighth week. It begins with the implantation of the zygote into the wall of the uterus. Most of the cell divisions, as well as the formation of all organs, take place during this stage.

The last stage is the fetus; it lasts from the eighth week until birth which occurs about 40 weeks after conception. This period is distinguished by quantitative growth. The fetus can now respond to the most basic kinds of stimulation.

 Trace development from the period of the embryo to the fetus.

 Embryonic growth begins when the zygote implants itself in the wall of the uterus. The embryo secretes enzymes and has tentacle-like growths called "villi" which enable it to attach to the uterus lining. Here we have the beginning of the placenta – a flat membrane that links the embryo to the mother and enables the embryo to derive nourishment from the mother. The embryo's wastes are also excreted through the placenta. Eventually, a structure called the umbilical cord, a long thick cord that attaches the fetus to the mother, begins to assume the function of the placenta.

By the end of the first month, the embryo is less than one inch long and weighs less than one ounce. Massive cell differentiation has occurred and organs are beginning to develop. The beginnings of the eyes, ears, and nose can be discerned.

By the end of the second month, the embryo can be recognized as a human being. Arm and limb buds and external genitalia are visible. All organs are present at this point and the entire embryo has curled itself. Although a great deal happens during this phase, there is little quantitative growth. The embryo at the end of its stage measures between 1 1/2 - 2 inches and weighs less than two-thirds of an ounce.

An outline of *what* develops *when* during the prenatal period is as follows:

| Approximate prenatal week | Development |
|---|---|
| 2nd week | Implantation on uterine wall. |
| 3rd – 4th week | Heart begins to pump. |
| 4th week | Digestive system begins to form. Eyes begin to form. |
| 5th week | Ears begin to form. |
| 6th week | Arms and legs first begin to appear. |
| 7th – 8th week | Male sex organs form. Fingers form. |
| 8th week | Bones begin to form. Legs and arms move. Toes form. |

| 10th – 11th week | Female sex organs form. |
| 12th week | Fetus weighs about one ounce. Fetal movement can occur. Fingerprints form. |
| 20th week | Mother feels movement. Reflexes – sucking, swallowing, and hiccuping appear. Nails, sweat glands, and soft hair developing. |
| 27th week | Fetus weighs about two pounds. |
| 38th week | Fetus weighs about seven pounds. |
| 40th week | Full-term baby born. |

**Teratogens** are any agents that may cross the placental barrier from mother to embryo/fetus, causing abnormalities. What abnormalities occur depend on what is developing prenatally as well as what the harmful agent is. Possible teratogens include maternal diseases (viruses), diet, drug use (including alcohol and nicotine), exposure to X-rays, medications (such as hormones), and other environmental influences. For instance, **fetal alcohol syndrome** (i.e., flattened nose, underdeveloped upper lip, widely spaced eyes, small head, mental retardation) can occur as a result of alcohol consumption during pregnancy.

Because so many vital organs and body parts are developing during the **embryo stage**, harmful agents are especially dangerous during this prenatal period. This is often referred to as a **critical period** in development. A critical period is any time during development that some developmental process must occur or it never will. For example, if something interferes with legs developing or forming prenatally, they will not develop or be formed later.

## Problem Solving Examples:

 Trace the development of the fetus from the beginning of the fetal stage through birth.

**A** The fetal period begins between the eighth and ninth week after conception. By the end of the third lunar month, the fetus measures 10 centimeters in length and weighs between three and four ounces. The head comprises about one-third of its entire length.

At this stage in its development, the fetus exhibits various types of movement and can respond to tactile stimulation. The fetus can arch its trunk or extend its head when touched. Fingernails and eyelids are now beginning to form. The sex is now distinguishable.

After the fourth month, the fetus measures 18 centimeters in length and has completed major development: all of the organs are discernible, the bones have begun to form, the hands can move and grasp, and hair is beginning to grow. Although the fetus is capable of some of the basic kinds of movement, it is not until the fifth month that the mother can feel these movements. The first feeling of fetal movement is called "quickening."

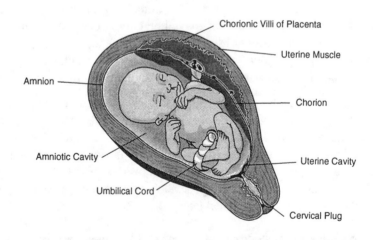

**Diagram of advanced fetus shows its membranes
and their relationship to the uterus.**

During the fifth month, a soft downy covering called the "laguno" forms over the fetus. The laguno usually grows over the entire body of the fetus and is shed during the seventh month. However, sometimes part of the laguno is present at birth, especially on the baby's back. By the end of the fifth month the fetus is 25 centimeters long and weighs about 9 ounces. Intrauterine movement becomes apparent. Sweat glands begin to develop and the formation of the hair and nails undergoes further development. It is important to note that until this time, the fetus would have had little chance for survival were it born prematurely. If the fetus survives until the twenty-eighth week, its chances for survival outside of the mother's womb are good.

By the end of the seventh month, the mother can give birth and the fetus will survive, although two more months of intrauterine development are desirable.

By the end of the sixth month, the fetus is approximately a foot long and weighs about 20 ounces. Most of the physiological developments have already taken place. From this point until birth, development is primarily quantitative.

 What are teratogens? List some examples and describe what effect they have on the developing fetus.

Teratogens are environmental agents that produce abnormalities in the developing fetus. A teratogen can be a disease a woman contracts during pregnancy, a chemical (drug or hormone) an expectant mother takes, or the radiation to which a pregnant woman may be exposed.

Diseases that can produce harmful effects on the fetus include German measles or rubella, mumps, polio, influenza, and toxemia (blood poisoning). Much attention has been given to the development of rubella during pregnancy since it is the most widespread of all the teratogenic diseases. Rubella can cause heart defects, cataracts, deafness, and mental retardation in the child. Toxemia can cause premature birth, resulting in babies who are smaller than average or it can lead to anoxia, a condition that prevents oxygen from reaching the child's brain. Anoxia can cause epilepsy, mental deficiency and behavior disorders.

Mumps, polio, and influenza produce teratogenic effects but these are not as serious as rubella and toxemia.

Within the past twenty years, research has found several drugs to have harmful effects on the developing fetus. These drugs include insulin, tolbutamide, thalidomide, aspirin (large doses), nicotine, heroin, morphine, methadone, and LSD (although research on LSD has been inconclusive). Pregnant women who are addicted to heroin, morphine, or methadone produce offspring who are also addicted to the drug. Withdrawal symptoms in these children are evident soon after birth. These symptoms include fever, tremors, convulsions, breathing difficulties, and intestinal disturbances. The mother's intake of insulin, tolbutamide (both used for diabetes), and thalidomide can cause various deformities in the fetus. Abuse of the first two drugs can result in death. Excessive intake of aspirin can cause growth retardation and lead to fetal abortion. Nicotine from cigarette smoking increases the fetus' heartbeat; however, there is presently no conclusive evidence indicating that smoking causes permanent damage to the heart or circulatory system.

Radiation is the third major type of teratogen. Two sources of radiation are X-rays and nuclear explosions. Large doses of therapeutic radiation have been found to cause spontaneous abortion, defects in the central nervous system, and mental retardation. The bombings of Japan during World War II have shown the effects of nuclear radiation on the unborn child. Pregnant women who were near the explosions gave birth to children that had one or more abnormalities such as dislocated hips, malformed eyes, heart disease, leukemia, and mental retardation. In the case of both therapeutic and nuclear radiation, exposure is most damaging if it occurs during the first twenty weeks of pregnancy.

## 1.1.2 Perceptual Development

The five senses, although not fully developed, are functional at birth. For instance, infants can **hear** as early as seven weeks before delivery. Shortly after birth, newborn infants or **neonates** appear capable of discriminating between sounds of different duration, loudness, and pitch. Newborns also appear to prefer the sound of a human voice. By six months of age, infants can discriminate between any two basic sounds used in language. In fact, they can make distinctions between sounds that older children and adults can no longer make because these sounds are not heard in their spoken language.

The sense of **smell** is also well developed in the newborn. By six weeks of age, infants can smell the difference between their mothers and strangers. In one study, infants as young as five days old were able to discriminate the breast pads of their mothers from those of other women on the basis of odor.

Infants respond to the four basic **tastes** (sweet, sour, salty, and bitter), but they usually prefer sweet.

Infants are also responsive to **touch**. Some research has shown that female infants may be more sensitive to touch than males. One area of study related to touch in young infants is the study of reflexes.

A number of **reflexes** (involuntary responses to stimuli) can be elicited in newborn infants. All healthy newborns exhibit them and many of these reflexes will disappear with age. For example, healthy newborn infants will blink when a light shines in their eyes. This reflex does not disappear with time. But other reflexes, such as the **Moro** (extension of arms when infant feels a loss of support), **Palmar** (hand grasp), and **Rooting** (turns toward object brushing cheek and attempts to suck) will disappear over the course of the first year of life.

At birth, neonates can see although their **visual acuity** is very poor (about 20/400 to 20/800 compared to average adult visual acuity of 20/20). Newborn infants can focus best on objects that are about nine inches away. They can also follow a moving object. Young infants also prefer to see the human face and other visual stimuli that have contour, contrast, complexity, and movement. By the time infants can crawl, they indicate that they have **depth perception** by refusing to crawl across the deep side of a **visual cliff**.

## Problem Solving Example:

 Describe the perceptual ability of the infant. Define "visual cliff."

Contrary to previous notions, the newborn infant has several perceptual skills. With regard to vision, for example, it has been found that infants are sensitive to light intensity, patterns, and contours. The eyes of a newborn infant can follow a slowly moving object. Infants can also differentiate various sound pitches as well as certain odors and tastes.

Vision takes longer to develop than the other senses. When the infant first opens his eyes, his visual focus is relatively fixed at about 9 inches from the cornea – the approximate distance between him and his mother's face during nursing. Eye muscles are weak, hence, eye coordination is poor. The infant is unable to change the focus of his eyes until he is about 2 months of age and he cannot change the shape of his lens to bring near and far objects into focus until he is about four months old. The visual acuity of the average infant at five and a half months is 20/100. This means that an infant can see objects from 20 feet while an adult with normal vision can perceive the same objects 100 feet away. By the end of infancy at age 2, however, the child's visual acuity matches an adult's.

Depth perception seems to develop by 6-8 months at the same time that the infant begins to crawl. To determine the existence of depth perception in children a device called a "visual cliff" is employed. This device usually consists of a raised platform, a part of which is composed of glass that gives the illusion of a cliff. Depth perception is noted when the child refuses to crawl from the "solid" side of the platform onto the glass. This refusal to crawl "off the cliff" is prevalent in most infants even at their mothers' inducement.

Several studies have been conducted on visual preference in infants. These studies have shown that infants spend more time looking at certain stimuli than at others. For example, infants gaze more at moving objects than at stationary ones. Their eyes tend to focus on figures with patterns rather than on those of solid colors.

Infants can also detect the location of certain sounds. Different frequencies of sound have different effects on the child. A low intensity sound has a calming effect, while an extremely loud sound may elicit a violent response.

The neonate is also sensitive to odor. When presented with an unpleasant odor, the child will turn his face away.

Response to taste is slight in the infant, although after two weeks he shows a marked preference for sugar over salt.

Studies indicate that the neonate is able to tolerate a high level of normally painful stimulation. Hence, sensitivity to tactile stimulation is not great.

By the time the infant is six months old, his perception is quite sophisticated and very similar to that of an adult.

### 1.1.3  Motor Development

**Maturation** is a term used to describe a genetically programmed biological plan of development that is relatively independent of experience.

The **proximodistal principle** of development describes the center-outward direction of motor development. For instance, children gain control of their torso before their extremities (e.g., they can sit independently before they can stand).

The **cephalocaudal principle** describes the head-to-foot direction of motor development. That is, children tend to gain control over the upper portions of their bodies before the lower part (e.g., they can reach and grasp before they can walk).

**Developmental norms** describe the average age that children display various abilities.

The developmental norms for motor development are as follows:

| Age | Behavior |
| --- | --- |
| 0 – 2 months | While prone (on stomach), can lift head. |

| | |
|---|---|
| 2 – 4 months | While prone, can hold chest up. |
| 2 – 5 months | Can roll from side to back. |
| 3 – 4 months | Will reach for objects. |
| 5 – 8 months | Sits without support. |
| 5 – 10 months | Stands holding on to objects. |
| 8 – 10 months | Crawls. |
| 6 – 10 months | Pulls self up to stand. |
| 7 – 13 months | "Cruises" – walks by holding on to objects. |
| 11 – 14 months | Walks alone. |
| 14 – 22 months | Walks up stairs. |

## 1.2 Social Development

Children also grow socially as they develop.

### 1.2.1 Temperament

**Temperament** refers to a child's characteristic mood and activity level. Even young infants are temperamentally different from one another.

**The New York Longitudinal Study** (1956), carried out by **Stella Chess**, **Alexander Thomas**, and **Herbert Birch**, was one of the first research projects that investigated temperament.

A **longitudinal** study is one that repeatedly observes and follows up the same group of individuals as they mature. For example, a group of children could have their temperament assessed when they are three months old, and again when they are two years old, five years old, and 10 years old.

A **cross-sectional** study studies different groups of individuals who are at different ages at the same point in time. A group of three–month–olds, two–year–olds, and five–year–olds may be assessed for temperament. In cross-sectional studies, therefore, the same individuals are not retested but instead are measured only once and group averages are used to demonstrate developmental changes.

The New York Longitudinal Study followed 140 children from birth to adolescence. Thomas, Chess, and Birch interviewed parents when the infants were between two and three months of age and rated the infants based on **activity level, rhythmicity, approach/withdrawal, adaptability, intensity of reaction,** and **quality of mood**. Thomas et al. found that they could classify infants into different groups based on temperament:

| | |
|---|---|
| **Easy Infants** (40%) | Adaptable to new situations. Predictable in their rhythmicity or schedule. Positive in their mood. |
| **Difficult Infants** (10%) | Intense in their reactions. Not very adaptable to new situations. Slightly negative mood. Irregular body rhythms. |
| **Slow-to-warm–up Infants** (15%) | Initially withdraw when approached, but may later "warm up." Slow to adapt to new situations. |
| **Average Infants** (35%) | Did not fit into any of the above categories. |

Thomas et al. found that temperament was fairly stable over time. For instance, they found that 70% of the difficult infants developed behavior problems during childhood, while only 18% of the easy infants did so. There were, of course, individual differences in whether specific children showed continuity or dramatic changes in their temperament over time. This early research has been criticized for relying exclusively on parents' subjective reports. However, more recent research that combines parents' reports with the reports of neutral observers and laboratory tests confirm the notion that there are clear temperamental differences among infants.

Although early temperament appears to be highly biologically determined, environment can also influence temperament. Researchers have used the term **goodness of fit** to describe an environment where an infant's temperament matches the opportunities, expectations, and demands the infant encounters.

## 1.2.2  Attachment

**Attachment** is the close emotional relationship between an infant and her or his caretakers.

Initially, infants attempt to attract the attention (usually through crying, smiling, etc.) of no one in particular. Eventually infants develop the ability to discriminate familiar from unfamiliar people. Shortly thereafter, they may cry or otherwise become distressed when preferred caregivers leave the room. This is referred to as **separation anxiety**. Separation anxiety may begin as early as 6 months of age, but it usually peaks around 18 months and then gradually declines.

**Mary Ainsworth** and her colleagues found they could distinguish three categories of attachments based on the quality of the infant-caregiver interactions.

*Secure Attachments* — Children use parent as **secure base** from which they explore their environment. They become upset if parent leaves the room but are glad to see the parent when parent returns.

*Insecure Attachments*

**Anxious-Ambivalent** — Tend not to use parent as a secure base (and may often cling or refuse to leave parent). They become very upset when parent leaves and may often appear angry or become more upset when parent returns.

**Avoidant** — These children seek little contact with parent and are not concerned when parent leaves. Usually avoid interaction when parent returns.

Parents of securely attached infants are often found to be more sensitive and responsive to their child's needs.

Some studies have found a relationship between attachment patterns and children's later adjustment. For instance, one study found that securely attached infants were less frustrated and happier at two years of age than were their insecurely attached peers.

Some researchers have suggested that temperament, genetic characteristics, and "goodness of fit" may be important for both the type of attachment bond formed and a child's later developmental outcome.

### 1.2.3 Parenting Styles

**Diana Baumrind** found that she could classify parents according to the following:

| | |
|---|---|
| **Authoritative Parents** | Affectionate and loving. |
| | Provide control when necessary and set limits. |
| | Allow children to express their own point of view – engage in "verbal give and take." |
| | Their children tend to be self-reliant, competent, and socially responsible. |
| **Authoritarian Parents** | Demand unquestioning obedience. |
| | Use punishment to control behavior. |
| | Less likely to be affectionate. |
| | Their children tend to be unhappy, distrustful, ineffective in social interactions, and often become dependent adults. |
| **Permissive Parents** | Make few demands. |
| | Allow children to make their own decisions. |
| | Use inconsistent discipline. |

High level of tolerance of the child's impulses and activities.

Their children tend to be immature, lack self-control, and explore less.

## 1.2.4 Day Care

Even though more children than ever before are now attending day care, there have been relatively few well-controlled studies that have looked at the effects of day care on development. Summarized below are the most consistent findings to date.

Children who attend day care usually score higher than children who do not attend day care on tests of **intelligence**. Non-day care children, however, usually catch up once they enter kindergarten and elementary school.

Children in day care tend to be more **socially skilled** – more cooperative, more confident, and better able to take the perspective of another.

Day care children also tend to be more **aggressive** and **noncompliant** (less likely to carry out an adult's request). Some have suggested this is because day care children have learned to think for themselves, not a symptom of maladjustment. It is also possible that children who are more aggressive or difficult to handle are more likely to be placed in day care by exhausted parents.

There is a slight tendency for day care children to be classified as **insecurely attached** (36% vs. 29% for home care children). Although statistically significant, some have questioned the practical significance of a 7% difference. This tendency for day care children to be classified as insecurely attached occurs mostly with infants who are placed in day care before 12 months, that is, during the period when initial attachments are forming.

## Problem Solving Example:

**Q** Define social development. Distinguish between work and play. List and define three types of play. How does play influence cognition?

**A** Social development refers to the development of behaviors the child engages in when he interacts with others. This area of study includes such topics as games, morality, learning the rules of society, and language acquisition.

Work and play are not distinguished by the specific activities they involve since these can be similar. Rather, work and play are distinguished by their end results. Play is engaged in for the pleasure – it is rewarding in and of itself. Work, on the other hand, is engaged in for the purpose of gaining a desired goal. Work can be enjoyable, but enjoyment is only incidental. The goal of most work is the attainment of monetary or material reward.

The child engages in three major categories of play: sensorimotor play, imaginative play, and parallel or cooperative play which is based on the existence of the interaction among the players. Sensorimotor play is engaged in during infancy. It involves the manipulation of objects. This manipulation provides the child with pleasurable stimulation. Sensorimotor play can consist of motor activities such as crawling, walking, running or waving.

Imaginative play involves games of make-believe. The child may imagine that he is someone or something else; or that the activities he engages in are something other than what they really are; or possibly he imagines that objects that he is playing with are something different than what they appear to be. Daydreaming is a major form of imaginative play. Daydreaming, however, involves no physical activity as compared to the other types of play. It is pure imaginative thinking.

The third type of play consists of two sequential types. Each is named and described in terms of the existence of interaction among the players. The first type, parallel play, begins shortly after infancy. Here, children play side by side but do not interact. They might use the same play materials but any sharing is unintentional. Between the ages of two and five, children begin to act out fantasies, pretending that they are various characters. When children find that they share knowledge of various characters or fantasies with one another, they engage in cooperative play as they act out fantasies together. Any type of play that involves interaction and cooperation among the players is called cooperative. One special type of cooperative play is called sociodramatic play. This type requires that the child's imagination and perception be highly active and alert - quick to pick up cues from the other players. It is comparable to the improvisation of professional actors. Through sociodramatic play, the child learns how to behave in society. In addition, the groundwork is laid for interpersonal relationships.

During the period of cooperative play, quarreling among players arises. This quarreling becomes especially common between the ages of three and four. Such quarreling marks the beginning of competitiveness, a quality which is highly reinforced in preschoolers in this culture.

In addition to teaching the child how to interact socially, play is also an influencing factor in cognition. Sutton-Smith (1967) considered play an activity in which the infant can work through new responses and operations and increase his range of responses. Sutton-Smith called play a mechanism for the "socialization of novelty." Children whose play is varied are given a chance to experience situations which increase their ability to respond appropriately to novel situations that may arise in the future. Children whose play is restricted are less able to respond in unfamiliar situations. Thus, play enlarges a child's repertoire of responses and thereby allows him to adjust quickly to new situations.

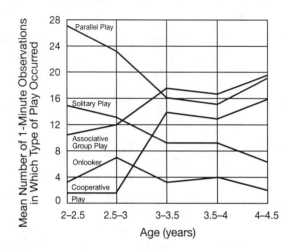

Changes in types of play as a function of age. Solitary, onlooker, and parallel play decrease, while associative and cooperative play increase.

## 1.3 Gender Role Development

**Gender roles** are our set of expectations about appropriate activities for females and males. Research has shown that even preschoolers believe that males and females have different characteristics. They also believe it is inappropriate to act like a member of the other gender.

Theories that explain gender role development include:

| | |
|---|---|
| **Social Learning Theory** | Proposes that children learn gender roles because they are **rewarded** for appropriate behavior and **punished** for inappropriate gender role behaviors. Children also watch and **imitate** the behaviors of others. |
| **Cognitive Theory** | **Kohlberg** argued that children learn about gender the same way that they acquire other cognitive concepts (see Piaget's theory described below). In the **gender labeling** $(2 - 3^1/2 \text{ yrs})$ stage, the child slowly becomes aware that he or |

she is part of a particular sex group. At this point the knowledge is little more than a label, like a personal name. In the **gender stability** ($3^1/_2 - 4^1/_2$ yrs) stage, children become more aware of the durability of their gender and can predict stereotypical roles later in life. However, children are still focused on the physical aspects of gender and believe that a physical change – such as donning the clothes of the opposite sex – can lead to a change in gender. Finally, between $4^1/_2$ and 7 years, gender consistency develops. In this stage children come to understand the permanency of gender.

**Psychoanalytic or Freud's Theory**

Freud's theory (see chapter 2) proposes that children establish their gender-role identity as a result of **identification with their same-sex parent** during the **Phallic stage**.

## 1.4 Cognitive Development

The most rapid cognitive development takes place during the first few years of life when the brain is growing rapidly. As the following sections on Piaget's theory and memory development indicate, however, cognitive development is best described as a life-long process.

### 1.4.1 Piaget's Theory

The Swiss researcher and writer **Jean Piaget** (1896 – 1980) spent most of his adult life describing the cognitive development of children. Although Piaget was never trained as a psychologist (his formal schooling was in biology and zoology), his theory of cognitive development has had a dramatic impact on how we view the abilities of children.

Piaget felt that cognitive development proceeded through four stages: the **sensorimotor stage** lasts from birth to approximately two years of age; the **preoperational stage** lasts from two to seven years of age; the stage of **concrete operations** covers the years seven to twelve; and finally, **formal operations**, extends from twelve years on.

According to Piaget, the order in which children pass through these stages is **invariant** or does not vary. The rate at which children pass through these stages does vary from child to child.

Piaget wrote that each stage of cognitive development represents a **qualitatively** different way of thinking. That is, children in each stage think differently from children in the other stages. Therefore, it is not just that children acquire more information as they grow older, but *how* they think actually changes with age.

Children pass from one stage to another as a result of **biological maturity** and **experiences** in their environment.

The major characteristics of each of these four stages follow:

### Sensorimotor Stage

Children "think" during this stage as a result of coordination of sensory input and motor responses. Because the child has not developed language, intelligence is nonverbal or **nonsymbolic** (the child cannot mentally represent objects or events). This stage is divided into **six substages** that outline how cognitive development proceeds during this stage. These six substages also represent the development of **object permanence**. Piaget was the first to suggest that infants lack object permanence – that is, they cannot mentally represent or think about objects that they are not directly interacting with (or, put another way, "out of sight, out of mind").

### Preoperational Stage

Preoperational thinkers can now **symbolize** or mentally represent their world. They can now think about objects that they are not interacting with at the present time. This period is dominated by a rapid development of **language,** which is a form of symbolic thinking. Children do have several limitations during this stage, however. These include **irreversibility** or the inability to mentally reverse a physical action to return an object to its original stage, **centration** (tendency to focus on one detail in a situation to the neglect of other important features), and **egocentrism** (inability to consider another's viewpoint). These three limitations are used to describe why preoperational children cannot solve **conservation tasks** (i.e., they do not understand that quantity cannot be judged by appearance alone). A preoperational child might believe that when you pour water from a tall, thin glass into a wide-mouthed, shorter glass, you have less water. The child centrates attention on the appearance of more water and cannot mentally reverse the operation and think about pouring the water back into the tall, thin glass.

## Concrete Operations

During concrete operations, children understand conservation. They understand, for example, that when water is poured from a tall, thin glass into a wide-mouthed, shorter glass, there is the same amount of water. Concrete operational children, therefore, can **decenter** their attention and understand **reversibility**. Concrete thinkers can also **arrange objects** according to size or weight and can **divide** something **into** its **parts**. **Mathematical operations** develop during this stage. Children are limited in this stage because thinking can only be applied to **concrete objects** and **events**, and they will have difficulty dealing with **hypothetical problems**.

## Formal Operations

**Formal operational** thinkers can handle **hypothetical problems**. They are, for instance, able to project themselves into the future and think about long-term goals. **Scientific reasoning** is also possible. That is, the ability to isolate a problem, review it systematically, and figure out all possible solutions is evident. The formal thinker is capable of understanding and appreciating the **symbolic abstractions** of algebra and literary criticism as well as the use of **metaphor** in literature. Formal operations, therefore, involve the development of **logical** and **systematic thinking**.

Other key terms from Piaget's theory include:

**Scheme** or **Schema**   Basic thought structures about what the world, objects, events, etc. are like.

**Organization**   Combining and integrating simple schemes.

**Adaptation**   The process by which a person changes to function more effectively in a given situation. Consists of **assimilation** and **accommodation**.

**Assimilation**   The process of applying an existing motor or mental scheme to various situations. Interpreting an event or experience based on our current scheme or thought structure. (For example, a child who calls all four-legged animals – even cats – "doggie." This child's current scheme seems to be that if you have fur and four legs, you are a dog.)

**Accommodation**   An ongoing process of refining motor or mental schema to fit the continually changing circumstances of one's environment. Changing or adjusting a scheme based on experience, understanding, etc. (e.g., the above mentioned child's dog scheme accommodates or adjusts to the notion that at least some four-legged animals are "cats").

Criticisms of Piaget's theory include his underestimation of children's cognitive abilities. Studies have shown that children are capable of performing many tasks (e.g., conservation) at earlier ages than Piaget predicted. Piaget also paid little attention to individual differences. Some aspects of his theory (e.g., formal operations) may be culturally specific.

## 1.4.2  Memory Development

Over the course of development, children use more and more sophisticated methods to remember, and their memory performance improves as a result. Although young infants (before three months of age) demonstrate memory capability when they recognize and remember familiar people, smells, objects, etc., in their environment, the use of intentional strategies for remembering have not been documented until around two years of age. These early strategies for remembering include **looking**, **pointing**, and **naming**.

By early elementary school, children are using **rehearsal** as a method for remembering. Rehearsal is a generic term for a variety of memory strategies that involve **repetition** as a method for remembering (e.g., repeating the phone number over and over until you dial it, writing your spelling words ten times each).

**Organization** or **clustering** strategies develop by late elementary school and involve the semantic grouping of materials into meaningful units (e.g., grouping spelling words by their prefix).

**Elaborative** strategies involve creating verbal or visual connections that add meaning to material and do not develop until adolescence or later. An example would be creating the phrase "Every good boy does fine" to remember that "e," "g," "b," "d," and "f" are the lines of the treble clef in music.

**Metamemory** is one's knowledge about memory, and it has been divided into **person** (everything we know about the memory abilities of ourselves and others), **task** (everything we know about memory tasks), and **strategy** (everything we know about techniques of learning and remembering) factors. As with strategy use, metamemory improves with age during childhood. At first, young children are unrealistic and make overly optimistic predictions about their memories (i.e., they believe they can remember everything) but with age they become more realistic in their expectations. They also know more about possible strategies for remembering with age.

## Problem Solving Examples:

Define Piaget's preoperational stage of cognitive development. Name and describe its two substages.

## Cognitive Development

**A** According to Piaget, a preschooler's cognitive
at the preoperational stage. The preoperational s.
of two substages: The preconceptual which lasts from ages ⸱
the intuitive thought which extends from ages 4 to 7.

---

### The Conceptual Period of Intelligence

| Stage | | |
|---|---|---|
| 1. Preoperational (2-7 yrs.) | a. Preconceptual (18 mos.-4 yrs.) | First such use of representational thought and symbols, such as words, for objects; classification of objects. |
| | b. Intuitive thought (4-7 yrs.) | Beginning of reasoning, but thinking is fragmented, centered on parts of things, rigid, and based wholly on appearances. |
| 2. Concrete operations (7-ll yrs.) | | Can perform mental operations and reverse them. Can add up "all the marbles." Operations are however confined to concrete and tangible objects that are immediately present. |
| 3. Formal operations (12-15 yrs.) | | Can form hypotheses, can go beyond appearances to deal with the truth or falsity of propositions. |

---

In contrast to the intelligence of an infant, a preschooler's intelligence allows him to internalize objects and events in his environment. Whereas an infant understands only what he immediately perceives and can perform activities only on objects immediately present, the preschooler employs symbolism. Symbolism includes the use of symbols and language to represent the world. The child can now think and speak of objects that are not immediately perceived. He develops concepts, actually "preconcepts," since they are not fully developed. These preconcepts, or the beginnings of cognitive thinking, enable the child to divide objects in the world on the basis of common properties. For example, a preschooler can recognize and name an elephant because of its massive size, gray color, floppy ears, and trunk. However, the preschooler cannot distinguish among different objects of the same class or animals of the same species. For example, a child who sees an elephant in a zoo and later sees another elephant in a circus would probably think that it was the same animal.

The child's reasoning ability during the preconceptual period can be divided into two types: transductive reasoning and syncretic reasoning.

Transductive reasoning occurs when the child bases his inferences on one particular occurrence or on a single attribute of an object. For example, a child might conclude that trucks and cars are the same objects since both have wheels. Likewise, if he sees a chicken lay an egg, he might assume that all animals lay eggs.

Syncretic reasoning reflects the child's constantly changing criteria for classification. This reasoning leads him to classify objects together that are disparate. For example, to distinguish among trucks, cars, and buses, the child would group all the trucks together. But he might also group blue cars with the trucks if one of the trucks is blue. He might also group some red trucks with the buses if some of the buses are red. Hence, the child's ever-changing criteria for classification lead to error.

The next substage of the preoperational stage is called intuitive thought. During this stage, the problem solving ability of the child is based upon his intuition or insight rather than on logical thinking. He is still dependent upon mental images since he is not yet able to see cause and effect relationships. Piaget demonstrated this theory through an experiment where he used a wire with three beads strung onto it. The beads were of three different colors: blue, red, and yellow. Holding the wire vertically, Piaget asked the child to note which colored bead was on top. Piaget then inserted the wire into a hollow cardboard tube and rotated it. As long as the child could imagine the position of the beads inside the tube, he could answer correctly, The child's perceptual capabilities are not developed sufficiently enough as yet, so as to enable the child to base his answer upon the relationship between an odd and even number of turns or half-turns.

Other characteristics of intuitive thinking include heavy reliance on perception and egocentric thinking.

An instance that reflects a preschooler's perceptually dominated thinking is exemplified when the child judges a tall and narrow pitcher to hold more orange juice than a short and wider one, despite the fact that both pitchers contain the same amount of liquid. An adult would be less apt to make such an error since his judgments are based on thought more than perception.

Although the child, during the preoperational period, is still somewhat limited in his intellectual ability, (i.e., intuitive rather than logical thinking), he is still capable of performing many tasks and is far ahead of the infant who possesses only sensorimotor intelligence.

 Discuss cognitive development during middle childhood as described by Piaget.

 According to Piaget's system of cognitive development, middle childhood is the period of concrete operations.

In Piaget's theory, an operation is a "thought." "Thought" refers to the mental representation of something that is not immediately perceived. During the period of concrete operations, the child is capable of invoking a mental representation or image of an object or an event, but this representation is linked to a mental image of the "concrete" perceptual experience. For example, if someone says the word car to a child in this stage, he will think of a time when he actually saw a car, rather than visualize an imaginary car, one that is divorced from his actual perception.

The period of concrete operations is also characterized by the acquisition of conservation. According to Piaget, conservation refers to the fact that only the addition or subtraction of a portion of an object changes it quantitatively, regardless of its appearance. For example, the child now knows that when a tall glass of water is poured into a smaller but wider glass, the amount of water remains the same. The child has learned to conserve. This stage of learning marks the dividing line between the periods of preoperational thought and concrete operations. The child is now using logical rather than intuitive thinking.

Three important rules of logic characterize a child's thinking during the period of concrete operations. These include identity, reversibility and combinativity. Identity means that there are certain activities that, when performed upon a particular object or situation, leave it unchanged. For example, blowing lightly on a glass of water does not alter it in any way. Reversibility refers to the fact that an operation can be undone. The child realizes that the water in the glass, which came from a pitcher, can be poured back into that pitcher. Combinativity is a logical law which states that several operations performed on a certain object or situation will yield a completely new object or situation. This law is also called closure. For example, if sugar is poured into a glass of water and then the water is stirred, a new substance, glucose, is produced. Related to combinativity is associativity or compensation. This term refers to the fact that several operations can be combined in different ways to produce the same end product. The child learns, for example, that the water in the glass can be disposed of in several ways: by pouring it down the sink, drinking it, letting it evaporate, etc.

In addition to acquiring a sense of conservation during the period of middle childhood, the child also learns classification. He is able to respond correctly when asked whether a bowl of mixed nuts contained more cashews or peanuts. He understands the concept of subclasses. He also comes to understand the concept of seriation – the arrangement of objects in a certain order following a particular standard. For example, a child during middle childhood would be able to arrange toys of different sizes in a line ranging from the smallest to the largest when asked to do so. In addition, he comes to understand the concept of number. During middle childhood he can comprehend the qualities of both ordinal numbers – numbers designating order (i.e., first, second, third, etc.), and cardinal numbers – numbers that designate quantity (i.e., one, two, three, etc.).

During the period of concrete operations, the child's thinking can deal with real objects and those that are easily imagined. He develops a simple system of logic which permits him to understand conservation. His intellectual development is far beyond that of the sensorimotor infant or the preoperational preschool child. Yet, his thinking is still not as sophisticated as that of the adolescent's whose cognitive development is at the stage of formal operations.

## 1.5 Erikson's Psychosocial Stages of Development

**Erik Erikson** proposed eight stages of social-emotional/personality development. He was one of the first theorists to discuss development throughout the life span – infancy through old age.

Erikson was trained as a psychoanalytic or Freudian theorist (see chapter 2). Erikson's theory, however, is very different from Freud's. For instance, Erikson believed that personality continues to develop over the entire life span (and not just childhood). Also, Erikson does not stress unconscious motives or desires. Like Freud, Erikson did feel that events that occur early in development can leave a permanent mark on one's later social-emotional development.

A description of Erikson's eight stages of psychosocial development follows. Each stage represents a specific task or dilemma that must be resolved.

**Trust versus Mistrust**
(First year of life)

Infant's needs must be met by responsive, sensitive caretakers. If this occurs, a basic sense of trust and optimism develops. If not, mistrust and fear of the future results.

**Autonomy versus Shame and Doubt**
(1 – 3 years)

Children begin to express self-control by climbing, exploring, touching, and toilet training. Parents can foster a sense of autonomy by encouraging children to try new things. If restrained or punished too harshly, shame and doubt can develop.

**Initiative versus Guilt**
(4 – 5 years)

Children are asked to assume more responsibility. Through play, children learn to plan, undertake, and carry out a task. Parents can encourage initiative by giving children the freedom to play, to use their imagination, etc. Children who are criticized or discouraged from taking the initiative, learn to feel guilty.

**Industry versus Inferiority**
(6 – 12 years)

In elementary school, children learn skills that are valued by society. Success or failure while learning these skills can have lasting effects on a child's feelings of adequacy.

**Identity versus Role Confusion**
(Adolescence)

The development of identity involves finding out who we are, what we value, and where we are headed in life. In their search for identity, adolescents experiment with different roles. If we establish an integrated image of ourselves as a unique person, then we establish a sense of identity. If not, role confusion results and can be expressed by individuals withdrawing and isolating themselves from family and friends or by losing themselves in the crowd.

**Intimacy versus Isolation**
(Young Adulthood)

After establishing an identity, a person is prepared to form deep, intimate relationships with others. Failure to establish intimacy with others leads to a deep sense of isolation.

**Generativity versus Stagnation**
(Middle Adulthood)

An interest in guiding the next generation is the main task of middle adulthood. This can be accomplished through one's creative or productive work or through caring for children. If adults do not feel that they have assisted the younger generation, a sense of stagnation will result.

**Integrity versus Despair**
(Late Adulthood)

This is a time of looking back at our lives. If we believe, overall, our lives have been well spent, a sense of integrity develops. If not, a sense of despair over the value of one's life will result.

## Problem Solving Example:

**Q** List and describe Erikson's stages of psychosocial development.

**A** Erik Erikson, an American psychoanalyst, devised a comprehensive theory for explaining psychosocial development. He believes that human behavior and personality result from a combination of heredity and cultural influences. He divides development from birth to maturity into eight basic stages. Each stage consists of a crisis which indicates a major turning point in the individual's life. This conflict is usually one between individual instinct and the restraining forces of external institutions. The individual must decide between two alternatives – one that is beneficial and another that is detrimental. Success in development is dependent upon successfully choosing the right alternative.

Erikson's stages are: (1) trust vs. mistrust, (2) autonomy vs. shame (3) initiative vs. guilt, (4) industry vs. inferiority, (5) identity vs. identity confusion, (6) intimacy vs. isolation, (7) generativity vs. stagnation and (8) integrity vs. despair.

During the first stage, the basic crisis centers on the development of either trust or mistrust. An infant is almost completely dependent on others for the fulfillment of his needs. If these needs are consistently satisfied and if he receives love and stimulation with those he comes in contact with, he will develop a sense of trust, not only in others but in himself and in his ability to handle his needs. If, on the other hand, his needs are not satisfied regularly and he receives little love, attention and stimulation, he will develop a sense of mistrust. If the mistrust is severe, the child may become timid and withdrawn since he has given up hope of ever achieving his goals. Erikson believes that the development of a healthy personality is contingent upon the formation of a basic trust – the individual's belief that his existence is meaningful.

During the second stage of psychosocial development, the basic crisis is between establishing autonomy and dealing with doubt and shame. The child who has developed a healthy sense of basic trust begins to see himself as a separate and autonomous being capable of doing things for himself. He has now gained some control of his bodily functions. He begins to assert himself, as can be seen in his response when asked to do something – he'll often reply, "no." Erikson believes parents should allow small children to do some things for themselves and should encourage exploration so that the child can develop a sense of autonomy or separateness. In addition, parents should assist their child in acquiring bodily control in such activities as walking and bowel movement.

Erikson contends that if parents are overprotective of their child (i.e., if they don't let him do things for himself) and are over-demanding with regard to his bodily functions, the child will develop feelings of shame and self-doubt. He will be shameful of not living up to his parents' expectations and will doubt his ability to live as a free, autonomous being. Individuals who successfully pass through this stage develop into independent adults who are able to make decisions for themselves and guide their own lives.

The third stage of Erikson's theory occurs between the ages of four and five. This period is characterized by the formation of either initiative or guilt, the development of motor skills resulting in increased locomotion, increase in language development as well as imagination and curiosity. Curiosity is especially evident in the child as reflected by his interest in exploring his (and others') bodies and differences between males and females. Erikson maintains that this interest is part of an "infantile sexuality." This includes an attraction to the opposite-sexed parent (note Freud's influence). The parent's response to the child's curiosity is an important factor in determining the degree of confidence and initiative the child will develop. A basic sense of guilt emerges if the child receives a negative or indifferent parental response to his questions or if he finds himself in an environment with little to explore. He may become anxious about asking questions and thereby stifle his curiosity. A child who receives positive and attentive parental response will develop a sense of confidence and initiative. He will feel happy and secure about his curiosity and will be eager to explore his environment. Successful resolution of this "initiative vs. guilt" crisis enables the child to take initiative and use his imagination in adulthood. He is equipped to deal with new, unfamiliar situations without the restrictions that result from guilt feelings.

The fourth stage in Erikson's scheme, occurring between ages 6 and 11, hinges on the resolution of industry versus inferiority. A child develops a sense of industry if he receives attention and praise for various accomplishments. For example, his parents might praise him for drawing a picture well or receiving a good report card or his teacher might commend him for writing the best composition in the class. As a result of such reactions, the child will actively pursue various projects since feedback from others assure him he can successfully execute them. In contrast, a child who fails consistently at various tasks or who receives little or no attention and praise develops a sense of inferiority. He avoids tackling new projects because he feels he will not handle them successfully. He puts little effort and enthusiasm into his work because he believes he is bound to fail. A child who successfully resolves this crisis and develops a sense of industry will come to find enjoyment in his work and will experience a sense of pride in his accomplishments. This attitude is carried into adulthood.

During this stage the child comes to define himself and others in terms of occupations – doctors, lawyers, teachers. The child defines his future self in terms of one such occupation.

Erikson's fifth stage of psychosocial development occurs during puberty. The major problem in this stage is the identity crisis (identity vs. identity confusion). The adolescent keeps asking, "Who am I?" Confusion about his role can cause him much stress and anxiety.

According to Erikson, the adolescent is very fickle about his self-image. This is reflected in constant fluctuations in preferred tastes and in styles of dress and haircut.

In an effort to offset confusion and allay some anxiety, the adolescent may align himself with an individual or group that can provide simple answers to his questions. In his quest for stability, he may devote himself to the guidelines of a teenage gang, a religious group, or a political organization. Adopting a life-style defined by others and living by others' codes may, however, produce some resentment. He may come to feel that he wants to do what *he* wants. If, however, the adolescent can't decide what he wants to do, he returns to the identity crisis.

Resolution of the identity crisis occurs when the adolescent receives support from others and is encouraged to seek answers to questions on his own. If he experiments with various life-styles, he will eventually find one that best suits him. In some cultures, such experimentation usually lasts until the individual reaches his mid-twenties. Successful resolution of the identity crisis results in a positive identity wherein the individual is confident of himself and his life-style.

The sixth stage of Erikson's plan is young adulthood. The basic crisis of this period is intimacy vs. isolation. At this time, the individual is concerned with establishing intimate, long-term relationships with others. If he has successfully resolved the identity crisis, he will be open and warm toward others, willing to share parts of himself and respond to others who wish to share themselves with him. If the identity crisis is not resolved, he will not be willing to open himself up to others. A person with an uncertain or unhealthy identity will not want to share himself with others. Erikson believes that individuals who refrain from intimate relationships do so because they fear the emotional risks involved. To support his statements, he points to hermits who elude intimacy to avoid being hurt and to pseudo-intimates who have many superficial friends but never let anyone get close enough for intimacy to develop. Successful resolution of the crisis in young adulthood leads to a healthy intimacy with another. A successful marriage is evidence of this.

The seventh stage of psychosocial development is adulthood. Here, concern for the next generation is of major concern. Having passed the stage of intimacy and concern for only a close few, the individual becomes preoccupied with his children and community. Through such active concern he avoids stagnation because he receives new stimulation in return. Hence, the basic crisis of this stage is generativity vs. stagnation. Success in resolving this crisis is evident in someone who takes an active role in parental guidance of the next generation and in community affairs.

The eighth and final stage of Erikson's scheme is maturity. The basic crisis during this stage is integrity vs. disgust and despair. A sense of integrity develops if the individual, having looked back on his life, believes it has been meaningful and relatively successful. He feels good about his past and is prepared to live the rest of his life in peace. A feeling of disgust, however, may arise if the individual sees his life as meaningless, wasted, and generally unsuccessful. He will feel despair if he believes it is too late to change or that his personality is so rigid that he can never change it.

## 1.6 Kohlberg's Theory of Moral Development

**Lawrence Kohlberg** developed a model of moral development based on an individual's responses to moral questions called **moral dilemmas**.

Kohlberg's theory attempts to explain how children develop a sense of **right or wrong**. Kohlberg was influenced by **Piaget's** theory and therefore felt that moral development was determined by cognitive development. The figure on page 37 charts an example of Kohlberg's theory.

Kohlberg's theory describes how individuals pass through a series of **three levels of moral development**, each of which can be broken into **two sublevels**, resulting in a total of **six stages**.

## Level I. Preconventional Morality

**Stage 1.  Punishment orientation**  A person complies with rules during this stage in order to avoid punishment.

**Stage 2.  Reward orientation**  An action is determined by one's own needs.

## Level II. Conventional Morality

**Stage 3.  Good-girl/Good-boy orientation**  Good behavior is that which pleases others and gets their approval.

**Stage 4.  Authority orientation**  Emphasis is on upholding the law, order, and authority and doing one's duty by following societal rules.

## Level III. Postconventional Morality

**Stage 5.  Social contract orientation**  Flexible understanding that people obey rules because they are necessary for the social order but that rules can change if there are good reasons and better alternatives.

**Stage 6.  Morality of individual principles orientation**  Behavior is directed by self-chosen ethical principles. High value is placed on justice, dignity, and equality.

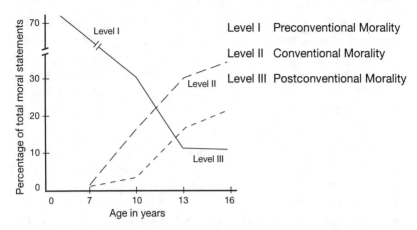

**Mean percent of moral statements on Kohlberg's
three levels made by boys aged 7 to 16**

Criticisms of Kohlberg's theory of moral development include that it may be better at describing the development of male morality than of female morality, and development may not be as orderly and uniform as his theory suggests. For instance, it is not unusual to find individuals who are reasoning at several adjacent levels of moral reasoning at the same time. Also, Kohlberg's theory describes moral reasoning but does not predict moral behavior.

## Problem Solving Example:

 Discuss the theory of Kohlberg (1964) on the moral development of the child during middle childhood.

Kohlberg believes that morality is a decision-making process rather than a fixed behavioral trait. In Freudian terms, morality reflects the strength of the ego which makes compromising decisions between the id and the superego. Based on this idea, Kohlberg devised a sequential design to explain the development of morality. The emergence of morality consists of three levels. Each level consists of two stages of moral orientation.

The first level is called preconventional morality. During the first stage of this level, the child believes that evil behavior is that which is punished and good behavior is that which is not punished. For the child, moral behavior is based on its subjective consequences. The second stage of level I is based on rewards. The child sees good as something that is pleasant and desirable, and evil as something that is unpleasant and undesirable. This level of morality is characteristic of the infant and preschooler.

The second level of morality is called conventional morality. At this level one finds that peer and social relations are important to the child. The first stage involves the type of morality that will win approval from parents, teachers, and peers. In other words, the child recognizes good moral behavior as that which is praised by society. The second stage of this level refers to a conformity to laws or to authority figures. Good behavior is characteristic of someone who obeys authority and society's laws. Both of these orientations reflect the child's desire to win acceptance and approval and to maintain good relations with whomever he comes in contact. This level characterizes the morality of the child during middle childhood.

The third and highest level of morality according to Kohlberg's scheme is called post-conventional or principled. This level initiates the beginning of the individual's moral standards. The child arrives at an understanding of individual rights, ideals and principles. He can see beyond the literal interpretation of rules and laws. He can perceive and distinguish between those laws that are good and those laws that are faulty. He recognizes democratic principles. An understanding of individual rights and democratically accepted laws are characteristic of the first stage of this level. The second stage reflects individual principles of conscience. The child develops notions of right and wrong which take precedence over the more primitive ways of judging behavior that was found in the first two levels. This type of morality is characteristic of the adolescent.

The development of morality is part of the process of socialization; that is, the learning of behavior that is appropriate and inappropriate for a particular culture. In addition, moral development is related to intellectual development. The child cannot develop a moral system until certain intellectual abilities have developed.

## 1.7 Adolescence

**Adolescence** is that time in development that occurs between childhood and adulthood.

*Physical Changes*: **Puberty** refers to rapid physical growth that occurs with hormonal changes that bring sexual maturity. **Secondary sex characteristics** (the physical features associated with gender but not directly involved in reproduction, such as male facial hair) emerge at this time. **Menarche** refers to girls' first menstrual period.

The peak growth spurt during puberty occurs earlier for girls than for boys.

*Social Concerns*: The main task for adolescents is to establish an identity. Adolescents are in **Erikson's identity versus role confusion** stage. Adolescents enter what Erikson called a **psychosocial moratorium**, which relates to the gap between the security of childhood and the autonomy of adulthood, where a person is free from responsibilities and can experiment with different roles.

At the turn of the century, psychologist **G. Stanley Hall** characterized adolescence as a time of **storm and stress**. Current research suggests that most adolescents make it through this time without any more turmoil than they are likely to encounter at other points in their lives.

*Cognitive Skills*: Cognitively, adolescents begin entering **Piaget's stage of formal operations**. **Imaginary audience**, a manifestation of adolescent egocentrism, may occur in which the teenager displays an unjustified belief that he or she is the focus of other people's attention.

## Problem Solving Example:

Briefly describe motor development in the adolescent.

One of the most notable characteristics of the adolescent's motor development is his increased physical strength. The strength results from his rapid growth ("the growth spurt") and his large amount of physical activity.

Boys, in particular, experience a rapid increase in the length of their limbs. This is sometimes disadvantageous since it can cause clumsiness in movement. However, these problems are eventually solved as the youngster becomes accustomed to his growing body and learns to use precision and smoothness in motor activities. The development of this quality is shared by all adolescents. The adolescent's speed of motor performance is greatly accelerated from middle childhood onward. The adolescent acquires keener senses and his reaction time is shorter. Participation in sports aids the development of physical strength and agility and improves reaction time.

## 1.8   Adulthood

Certain events mark adult attainment in our society. Such events include leaving one's family, supporting oneself, getting married, and having children. Many of these transitions into adulthood involve changes in family relationships and responsibilities.

### 1.8.1   Early Adulthood

**Early adulthood** extends from approximately 20 to 40 years of age.

*Physical Changes*: Reaction time and muscular strength peak in the early to mid-twenties. External signs of aging begin to show in the 30s when the skin loses elasticity and hair becomes thinner and begins to turn gray.

A gain in weight is common because a lowered metabolic rate contributes to increased body fat relative to muscle.

*Social Concerns*: Social development during early adulthood is focused on forming intimate relationships. Individuals are in **Erikson's intimacy versus isolation** stage.

*Cognitive Skills*: Intellectual abilities and speed of information processing are relatively stable and gains in intellectual skills are possible during early adulthood. Some studies have shown that approximately 50% of all adults have reached Piaget's stage of **formal operations**.

### 1.8.2 Middle Adulthood

**Middle adulthood** lasts from approximately 40 to 65 years of age.

*Physical Changes*: During middle adulthood the number of active brain cells declines, but the significance of this loss is unclear. In vision, farsightedness increases. Sensitivity to high-frequency sounds decreases. In women, **menopause** (ending of monthly menstruation) occurs at around 51 years of age. The **male climacteric** includes decreased fertility and decreased frequency of orgasm. For both sexes, sexual activity declines although capacity for arousal changes only slightly.

*Social Concerns*: Over time, individuals become more aware of their own mortality and the passage of time and enter **Erikson's generativity versus stagnation** stage. Those in middle adulthood are often caught between the needs of their children and those of their own aging parents and are thus referred to as the **sandwich generation**.

There has been much debate concerning whether or not most people go through a **mid-life crisis**. Many studies have failed to find increased emotional turbulence at mid-life.

*Cognitive Skills*: Effectiveness of retrieval from long-term memory begins a slow decline but is often not noticeable until after age 55. Despite a decreased speed in cognitive processing, intelligence and problem-solving skills usually remain stable. Career development peaks.

## 1.9 Aging

**Gerontologists** study aging.

**Ageism** refers to prejudice against older people.

*Physical Changes*: **Biological aging** is a gradual process that begins quite early in life. Peak physical functioning occurs around 25 years of age and gradually declines thereafter. The rate of aging is highly individualized. The sensitivity of vision, hearing, and taste decreases in the elderly (those aged 65 and older). Height and weight decreases are also common. The risk of chronic diseases (heart disease, stroke, cancer, etc.) increases. Slower reaction times are common.

*Social Concerns*: **Elderly adults** are in **Erikson's stage of ego integrity versus despair** and accordingly will be engaged in a **life review**.

*Cognitive Skills*: A **terminal decline** in intellectual performance occurs in the two to three years that precede an elderly adult's death. **Senile dementia** is an abnormal deterioration in cognitive abilities. **Alzheimer's disease** is a form of dementia.

## Quiz: Human Development

1. The order of the three stages of prenatal development, from beginning to end are

    (A) embryo, fetus, germinal.

    (B) ovum, embryo, fetus.

    (C) germinal, embryo, fetus.

    (D) Both (B) and (C).

2. During prenatal development, the ears form

    (A) in the third week.

    (B) in the fifth week.

    (C) in the seventh week.

    (D) at the end of the first trimester.

3. By what age should an infant be able to discriminate between any two basic sounds used in language?

  (A) Two months

  (B) Four months

  (C) Six months

  (D) Eight months

4. The New York Longitudinal Study is a research project that investigated

  (A) temperament.

  (B) attachment.

  (C) parenting styles.

  (D) gender roles.

5. According to Diana Baumrind's classification system, parents who allow their children to express their own point of view and engage in "verbal give and take" are

  (A) permissive parents.

  (B) authoritarian parents.

  (C) authoritative parents.

  (D) bad parents.

6. What theory proposes that children learn gender roles because they are rewarded for appropriate behavior and punished for inappropriate gender role behaviors?

  (A) Social learning theory

  (B) Cognitive theory

(C) Social cognitive theory

(D) Freud's theory

7.  According to Piaget, during what stage/operation in cognitive development do children understand conservation?

    (A) Sensorimotor stage

    (B) Preoperational stage

    (C) Concrete operations

    (D) Formal operations

8.  At what age does a person experience the Industry versus Inferiority stage, according to Erik Erikson's eight stages of development?

    (A) 3-5 years

    (B) 6-12 years

    (C) Adolescence

    (D) Young Adulthood

9.  Kohlberg's theory attempts to explain how children develop a sense of

    (A) identity.

    (B) trust.

    (C) shame and doubt.

    (D) right or wrong.

10. The peak growth spurt during puberty occurs

    (A) earlier for girls than boys.

    (B) later for girls than boys.

    (C) around the same age for girls and boys.

    (D) There is no peak growth spurt.

## ANSWER KEY

| | | | |
|---|---|---|---|
| 1. | (D) | 6. | (A) |
| 2. | (B) | 7. | (C) |
| 3. | (C) | 8. | (B) |
| 4. | (A) | 9. | (D) |
| 5. | (C) | 10. | (A) |

# CHAPTER 2

# Personality

## 2.1  Psychodynamic Approach

**Personality** refers to distinctive, enduring characteristics or patterns of behavior. An individual's personality reveals itself through consistent behavior in a variety of situations.

This chapter describes different theories that have attempted to explain personality and its development.

**Psychodynamic theories** (also called **psychoanalytic theories**) of personality descended from **Sigmund Freud** and his theory of personality.

For most psychodynamic theorists, personality is mainly **unconscious**. That is, it is beyond our awareness. In order to understand someone's personality, the **symbolic** meanings of behavior and deep inner workings of the mind must be investigated. Early experiences with parents shape personalities, according to psychodynamic theorists.

### 2.1.1  Freud's Theory

**Sigmund Freud** (1856–1939) was a medical doctor from Vienna, Austria, who specialized in neurology. His psychodynamic approach to personality developed as a result of his work with adult patients who had psychiatric and emotional problems.

Freud's theory emphasized three main points:

1. Childhood experiences determine adult personality.

2. Unconscious mental processes influence everyday behavior.

3. Conflict influences most human behavior.

According to Freud, each adult personality consists of an **id**, **ego**, and **superego**.

| Personality component | When it develops | How it functions |
|---|---|---|
| **Id** | at birth | Pleasure principle. Unconscious instincts. Irrational. Seeks instant gratification. Contains the libido. |
| **Ego** | around 6 months | Reality principle. Mediates id and reality. Executive branch. |
| **Superego** | around 6 years | Morality principle. Personal conscience. Personal ideals. |

According to Freud, the **id** is unconscious and has no contact with reality. It works according to the **pleasure principle** – the id always seeks pleasure and avoids pain. The id contains the **libido** or sexual energy.

The **ego** evolves from the id and deals with the demands of reality. It is called the **executive branch** of personality because it makes rational decisions. The **reality principle** describes how the ego tries to bring individual id demands within the norms of society. The ego, however, cannot determine if something is right or wrong.

The **superego** is capable of determining if something is right or wrong because it is our conscience. The superego does not consider reality, only rules about moral behavior.

According to Freud, behavior is the outcome of an ongoing series of conflicts between the id, ego, and superego. Conflicts dealing with sexual and aggressive impulses are likely to have far-reaching consequences because social norms dictate that these impulses be routinely frustrated.

Freud considered personality to be like an **iceberg** – most of our personality exists below the level of awareness just as most of an iceberg is hidden beneath the surface of the water. Freud referred to the hidden part of our personality as the **unconscious**. Even though Freud felt that many thoughts, memories, and desires were unconscious, they nonetheless influence our behavior.

The **conscious** part of our personality consists of whatever we are aware of at any particular point in time.

The **preconscious**, according to Freud, contains material that is just below the surface of awareness but can be easily retrieved. An example of preconscious awareness would be your mother's birthdate. You were not thinking of your mother's birthdate but can if you need or want to.

The figure on the next page presents the iceberg analogy of Freud's notions of unconscious, conscious, and preconscious and how they relate to the three structures of personality (id, ego, and superego).

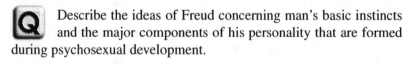

## Problem Solving Example:

**Q** Describe the ideas of Freud concerning man's basic instincts and the major components of his personality that are formed during psychosexual development.

**A** According to Sigmund Freud, man has two basic urges or tendencies. One is survival, the other is procreation. Freud was most interested in the reproductive urge since this one is always being

Freud's Model of Personality

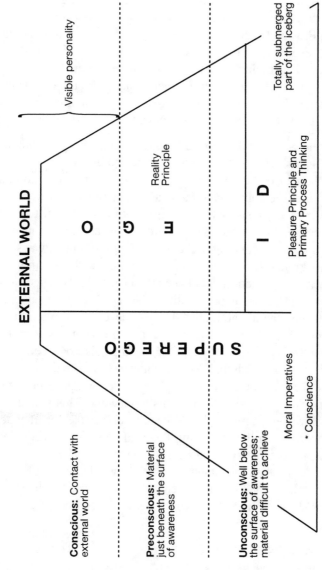

**Conscious:** Contact with external world

**Preconscious:** Material just beneath the surface of awareness

**Unconscious:** Well below the surface of awareness; material difficult to achieve

Visible personality

**EXTERNAL WORLD**

O
G
E
I
D

SUPEREGO

Reality Principle

Pleasure Principle and Primary Process Thinking

Totally submerged part of the iceberg

Moral Imperatives

* Conscience

**Freud's iceberg analogy of personality illustrates his belief that most personality processes occur below the level of conscious awareness.**

thwarted by the environment. He coined the term "libido" as the source of energy for the sexual urge. It is important to note that Freud considered several behaviors to be sexual in nature, not just the act of sex itself. Activities such as smoking and thumbsucking were considered by Freud to be sexual. He later defined two instincts in man which he called Eros and Thanatos. These are Greek terms that mean love and death, respectively. Eros is the life instinct or the will to live which includes the libidinal urges. Thanatos refers to the death wish or the death instinct. These two urges, according to Freud, compete against each other. It is the life-giving urges of Eros that are most intimately connected with the child's development.

Freud sees the newborn infant as a simple and selfish being. The infant's personality, he believed, is governed by the id. The id contains all of human being's instinctual urges. The infant has no ethical or moral rules; he demands immediate satisfaction of his wants. The infant is pure id – he only feels urges and knows they must be satisfied. He does not understand his environment; he has no idea that due to the nature of his surroundings, instant gratification is not always possible. He only knows, for example, that he is hungry and cries until he is fed. Hence, we have a conflict between the id and reality. This leads to the second level of human personality – the ego. The ego is the intermediary between the id and reality. The ego develops between the ages of eight months and eighteen months as the child acquires an understanding of what is possible. The ego also distinguishes between long-range and short-range goals and decides which activities will be most profitable to the individual. For example, a student might decide he would rather watch television than do his homework. This is a short-range goal. However, he might also realize the long-range goal that doing his homework rather than watching TV will further his education and possibly lead to a better occupation in the future. The ego in this case might choose the long-range goal since it would be most beneficial to the individual. The long-range benefits are preferred to immediate gratification. Thus, the id and ego work together to determine the individual's goals.

Eventually, the child acquires a moral sense. This is embodied in the third component of his personality called the superego. The superego represents the taboos and mores or rules of the society in which the child lives. It might encompass religious rules as well. The process by which the child comes to learn cultural norms is called socialization. Hence, the development of the superego represents socialization in the child.

The id and superego are often in conflict because fulfillment of many of the id's urges would require behavior that is socially unacceptable.

The superego develops from the ages of eighteen months to six years. It is often described as having two divisions. One is the conscience which consists of the child's internalized rules. The other is the ego ideal, which represents strivings and goals highly regarded by the parents.

**Defense mechanisms** are unconscious methods used by the ego to distort reality and thereby protect us from anxiety. Anxiety can result from the irrational, pleasure demands of the id or from the superego causing guilty feelings about a real or imagined transgression.

Common defense mechanisms are:

| | |
|---|---|
| **Rationalization** | Creating false but plausible excuses to justify unacceptable behavior. |
| | Example: Reducing guilt for cheating on your taxes by rationalizing "everyone does it." |
| **Repression** | Expelling disturbing wishes, thoughts, or experiences from conscious awareness. The feelings may remain conscious, but they are detached from the associated ideas. |
| | Example: Having no memory of an unpleasant experience. |
| **Reaction Formation** | Behaving in exactly the opposite of one's true feelings. |

Example: A mother who feels resentment toward a child may be overly cautious and protective.

**Regression**

Reversion to immature patterns of behavior.

Example: Temper tantrums.

**Projection**

Attributing one's own thoughts, feelings, motives, shortcomings, etc. to others.

Example: A wife who constantly suspects her husband of having an affair because unconsciously she has thought of having an affair.

**Displacement**

Shifting unacceptable feelings from their original source to a safer, substitute target.

Example: You are mad at your boss, but you do not yell at your boss; instead you become angry with a family member when you return home.

**Sublimation**

A useful, socially acceptable course of behavior replaces a socially unacceptable or distasteful impulse.

Example: A person who feels aggression due to a lack of control plays an aggressive game of basketball with friends every other day.

**Intellectualization**

By dealing with a stressful situation in an intellectual and unemotional manner, a person detaches himself from the stress.

Example: A person who has lost a family member due to illness will willingly speak of the medical terminology of the illness but will not discuss the emotional aspects of the illness.

**Denial**

An individual does not acknowledge some painful or anxiety-provoking aspect of reality or of the self.

Example: A person with severe stomach pains, possibly an ulcer, refuses to see a doctor because he feels it is only indigestion.

## Problem Solving Example:

 Define defense mechanism. List and describe some examples.

A defense mechanism is a process an individual employs to compensate for a desire that cannot be fulfilled because of social taboos. Defense mechanisms are created by the ego in an attempt to deal with the unfulfilled wish by mediating between the id and the superego. Often, the anxiety which results from conflict between the id and superego becomes excessive and the individual must find means of dealing with it. Defense mechanisms are these means.

Examples of defense mechanisms include repression, displacement, reaction-formation, intellectualization, projection, and denial.

Repression occurs when an individual experiences a painful incident or event and tries to forget it. He represses the experience by burying it in his unconscious mind. The unconscious mind is replete with repressed feelings toward painful experiences. An example of this is an adult who was once abused by a parent during childhood. The individual tries to forget about the parent or at least those occasions when the parent abused him.

Displacement results when an individual wishes to gratify a desire, but engaging in the activity that will fulfill his desire is socially unacceptable. Hence, the ego compromises and finds another means of gratification. The alternate activity may not be as pleasurable as the activity of his first choice, but it suffices for the time being. Very often, the desire is unconscious. For example, someone who has an angry encounter with his/her boss at work may be unable to act on his/her feelings of rage and hostility due to fear of losing his/her job. When he/she returns home from work he/she may pick a fight with his/her spouse or children as a way to, unknowingly, vent his/her anger and hostility stemming from the workplace conflict. Thus, one form of behavior is displaced for another.

Reaction-formation occurs when an individual is disturbed by his natural feelings toward a particular person, object or phenomenon. Because of the resulting anxiety, he consciously tells himself and others that he feels the opposite of his true feeling. For example, if a person fears he may be homosexual, he may constantly communicate to others that he is not. This may be done either verbally or by engaging in behavior exclusively appropriate for his or her own sex. A male who fears he is homosexual might engage in "manly" activities such as fighting or performing various feats of strength. Likewise, a female who fears lesbian tendencies might dress in an excessively feminine fashion – always wearing dresses, jewelry, or makeup. In addition, people who fear that they are homosexual frequently display reaction-formation by denouncing homosexuality and condemning those who are openly homosexual.

Intellectualization is also called rationalization. It occurs whenever an individual fears that a behavior he has engaged in might be abnormal. Hence, he searches for ways or excuses that will "rationalize" his behavior and make it appear perfectly normal. Intellectualization implies that the individual is primarily concerned with the intellectual or rational aspects of his behavior rather than the emotional aspects. For example, an obese person who refuses to diet, may insist that dieting is unhealthy and that he needs to eat as much as he does in order to sustain his energy level.

Projection is a defense mechanism where the individual projects or attributes his anxieties or abnormalities to other people. Returning to the example of homosexuality given for reaction-formation, a person who fears that he may be homosexual will overtly deny that he is.

In addition, he will call other people homosexual (even if they are not) in order to divert attention away from his own fears and allay his anxiety. Also, by calling others homosexual, he reduces the chances that other people will think he is one. Because the individual projects attributes he fears he has, he is displaying projection.

Denial, another defense mechanism, involves a distorted rather than objective view of the world. It often comes about when a person tries to make a particular behavior appear less abnormal or heinous by perceiving the world as a place where everyone or most people engage in the same behavior. Or he may perceive his society as being tolerant or praising of the behavior. For example, someone who always cheats on his taxes may deny that his behavior is wrong because "everyone else does it" or because the government asks for too much money which it doesn't deserve.

Defense mechanisms are defensive in that they protect individuals from anxiety they may not be able to tolerate. These mechanisms may be strong or mild depending on the individual and the anxiety-producing situation.

## 2.1.2 Stages of Psychosexual Development

Freud believed that we go through five stages of psychosexual development in forming our personalities. Each stage represents a different **erogenous zone** or part of the body where pleasure originates.

### Freud's Psychosexual Stages

| Stage | Age | Erogenous Zone | Description |
|-------|-----|----------------|-------------|
| **Oral** | 0 – 18 months | Mouth | Stimulation of mouth produces pleasure; enjoys sucking, biting, chewing. Weaning is major task or conflict. |
| **Anal** | 18 – 36 months | Anus | Toilet training is major task. Expelling and retaining feces produces pleasure. |

| Phallic | 3 – 6 years | Genitals | Self-stimulation of genitals produces pleasure. **Oedipal** (for boys) and **Electra** (for girls) conflicts occur – children have erotic desires for opposite-sex parent as well as feelings of fear and hostility for same-sex parent. Successful resolution of this conflict results in identification with same-sex parent. |
| --- | --- | --- | --- |
| Latency | 6 – 12 years | None | Sexual feelings are repressed. Social contacts beyond immediate family are expanded. |
| Genital | Puberty onward | Genitals | Establishing intimate, sexual relations with others is main focus. |

According to Freud, children experience conflicts between urges in their erogenous zones and societal rules. **Fixation** can result when these urges are either frustrated or overindulged in any one erogenous zone. Fixation results in one's personality becoming locked at a particular psychosexual developmental stage.

Freud felt that the first three psychosexual stages were the most important for personality development. Examples of possible personality traits resulting from fixations in the first three psychosexual stages are presented here.

| Stage | Examples of traits related to fixation |
| --- | --- |
| Oral | Obsessive eating
Smoking
Drinking
Sarcasm |

|        | Overly demanding |
|        | Aggressiveness |

Anal | Extreme messiness
| Overly orderly
| Overly concerned about punctuality
| Fear of dirt
| Love of bathroom humor
| Anxiety about sexual activities
| Overly giving
| Rebelliousness

Phallic | Excessive masturbation
| Flirts frequently
| Excessive modesty
| Excessively timid
| Overly proud
| Promiscuity

## Problem Solving Examples:

 List and describe Freud's stages of psychosexual development.

Freud divided the period of psychosexual development into five stages. These stages are characterized by the objects that are the goals of the individual during each particular stage. Freud believed that the primary driving force in an individual's life was the sexual urge. The stages are therefore especially concerned with representing changes of sexual gratification in relation to the child's body. The five stages in sequential order are: the oral phase, the anal phase, the phallic phase, a latency period, and the genital phase.

The oral phase begins at birth and lasts eight months. It is characterized by the infant's concern for his mouth and the gratification he seeks from oral stimuli. The most obvious oral activity the child derives pleasure from is eating. Oral stimulation, however, is also produced by engaging in such activities as sucking, biting, swallowing and manipulating various parts of the mouth. Freud contended that these activities are the child's means of fulfilling his sexual urges. Hence, Eros (the life instinct) makes its appearance. But Thanatos (the death instinct) is also seen since quite frequently children destroy objects they come in contact with, often by biting them.

During this phase, the child's personality is controlled by the id. He demands immediate gratification of his wants.

The next stage of psychosexual development is the anal phase when the child's central area of bodily concern is the rectum. Bowel movements become a source of pleasure to the child. He may defecate often to achieve this pleasure. This, however, would bring him into conflict with his parents. The conflict leads the child to develop an ego. He comes to realize that he cannot always do what he wants when he wants. He learns that there are certain times when it is appropriate to expel waste and other times when it is inappropriate. He gradually comes to understand his parents' wishes and abides by them.

The child's central interest gradually shifts again – this time to the genital region. This stage is called the phallic phase and lasts from approximately three years of age to six. Sexual gratification becomes more erotic during this time as evidenced by the child's masturbation: actual manipulation of the genitals.

It is during this stage that the phallus (male genital) acquires a special significance. Freud believed that the increased awareness in the male of his sexual organs leads him to subconsciously desire his mother. In addition, the male child grows envious and resentful of his father and wishes to replace him as the object of his mother's love. This situation is called the Oedipus Complex.

Similarly, a female undergoes a complex wherein she desires her father and rivals with her mother for her father's affections. This is called the Electra Complex. This complex involves penis envy on the part of the female child. She believes that she once had a penis but that it was removed. In order to compensate for its loss, Freud believed the girl wants to have a child by her father. Eventually, however, both the boy and the girl pass through these complexes. Once this happens, they begin to identify with the parent of their own sex. This marks the end of the phallic phase and the beginning of a new one.

The next period, the period of latency, is characterized by indifference to sexually related matters. During this time, the child's identification with the parent of his own sex becomes stronger. The child imitates his or her behavior – speech, gestures, mannerisms, as well as beliefs and value systems. The child also incorporates more and more of the beliefs and values of his culture. Thus, the superego is developing to a greater extent. (It began to develop during the late anal and the phallic stages.) The child comes to distinguish between acceptable and unacceptable behavior in his society.

The period of latency is also marked by the fact that children seek associations (or playmates) of their own sex. Boys prefer the company of boys and consciously avoid girls. Girls prefer contact with other girls and avoid boys. This period of sexual latency lasts five years, from ages six to eleven.

The final stage of motivational development is called the genital phase, which is the longest of the five stages. It lasts seven years from ages eleven to eighteen. This period is similar to the anal stage. There is a renewed interest and pleasure derived from excretory activity. In addition, masturbation takes place and is engaged in much more frequently at this time than during the anal stage.

In the beginning of the genital phase, the person seeks associations with members of his own sex just as in the latency period. But the associations are stronger in the genital phase and Freud believed they are homosexual in nature, even though homosexual activity may not take place. As this period progresses, however, the homosexual tendencies are supplanted by heterosexual ones and toward the latter part of this phase, the child makes contact and forms relationships with members of the opposite sex.

Also at this time, the superego undergoes further development and becomes more flexible. In the latency period the superego is quite rigid. The child adopts rules in the most literal sense. During the genital phase, the individual realizes that some rules are less vital than others. Consequently, his behavior will reflect this. He accepts some rules or norms and makes exceptions to others.

 Explain the terms fixation and regression as used by Freud in his descriptions of human development.

According to Freud, fixation and regression are the results of abnormal personality development. In his scheme of personality development consisting of different stages, Freud stated that there is a certain amount of frustration and anxiety as the individual passes from one stage to the next. If the amount of frustration and anxiety becomes too great, that is, if there is too much anxiety about moving to the next stage, development may halt and the individual will become fixated at one stage. An overly dependent child is an example of someone who is fixated. Development has ceased at an early stage of development preventing him from becoming independent.

In contrast, regression refers to a retreat to an earlier stage of development. Someone who encounters an intolerable experience and is unable to deal with it may engage in behavior appropriate to someone at an earlier stage of development. Often, regression is used as a means of handling frustration. A six-year-old who reverts to wetting his pants may be expressing his frustration from the loss of parental attention due to the birth of a new sibling. Similarly, a child who displays infantile behavior on his first day of school – crying, thumb sucking, etc. – is regressing.

Regression is usually determined by the earlier fixations of the individual. In other words, the person tends to regress to a stage upon which he has been previously fixated. For example, the child who becomes fixated at a certain stage which results in his overdependence, may become overdependent later in life when faced with an extremely unbearable or frustrating experience. In this case, he is regressing to a point of fixation.

It is important to keep in mind that fixation and regression are relative conditions. An individual rarely fixates or regresses completely. Usually most aspects of an individual's personality will mature normally, but his behavior may be characterized by infantilisms – childish conduct which results from frustrations. Fixation and regression are both related to abnormalities in personality development. Fixation refers to a halting of normal development, whereas regression refers to a return to earlier, less mature stages of development.

## 2.1.3 Neo-Freudians

**Neo-Freudians** are personality theorists who started their careers as followers of Freud but eventually disagreed on some of the basic principles of his theory.

Theorists include Carl Jung, Alfred Adler, and Karen Horney. They disagreed with the importance Freud placed on psychosexual development and the importance of childhood experiences on personality development. Though they believed childhood experiences do play a role in development, future goals in middle age are more important for personality development.

## 2.1.4 Evaluating the Psychodynamic Approach

Freud and neo-Freudians have contributed to our understanding of personality and personality development:

- They suggested that early experiences can shape our personality and that personality can best be understood by examining it developmentally.

- Freud encouraged psychologists to study human emotions and motivation.

- The concept of the unconscious is still valuable to many psychologists.

- They developed psychotherapies based on their theories. (See chapter 6.)

*Criticisms* of the psychodynamic approach include:

It is untestable. For example, ideas such as the unconscious are difficult to measure.

Data to support these theories often come from case studies of individual clients or from clients' memories. Memories may be flawed and therapists may see what they expect to see based on their theoretical orientation.

Freud's theory is pessimistic about human nature.

Freud's theory is sexist and biased against women.

## Problem Solving Example:

Discuss some criticisms of Freud's theory.

Freud's theories have been repeatedly attacked both by those outside the psychoanalytic circle and those psychoanalysts who differ from him on certain theoretical and practical points. Despite the large number of criticisms, Freud's theory still has a far reaching impact on modern psychology and psychotherapy.

The concepts that have been under fire most often have been his views on sex, the unconscious, and the critical determining character of early childhood experience. Because he was living and working in an age in which the mores were unusually strict concerning the expression of natural sexuality, his strong emphasis on sex has been seen by many to be a reaction to this repressive environment. Today, sex is seen as only one of many basic human needs. His assignment of sexual significance to early childhood experience has also suffered severe attack. Cross-cultural studies have failed to confirm the universality of the Oedipus Complex. Also, studies designed to test other hypotheses regarding early parent-child relations have proved inconclusive.

The psychoanalytic method has been criticized because the techniques of free association, dream analysis and transference demand that the patient be relatively healthy to start with, highly motivated to improve and quite skilled at expressing and interpreting his thoughts and feelings. It has also been demonstrated that the lengthy, costly process of psychoanalysis is no more effective than shorter, less costly procedures that are more widely applicable. Again, these criticisms have not prevented classical psychoanalysis from remaining the pre-ferred method of treatment for some mental health practitioners.

Whatever criticisms might be leveled at Freud, it cannot be denied that he is one of the great modern thinkers. His stimulating and com-pelling thinking process has served as a source of so much inspiration to students of human behavior that it is difficult to assess the size of his contribution to the study of human nature.

## 2.2  Behavioral Perspective

The **behaviorist perspective** is that personality is a collection of **learned behavior patterns**. Personality, like any other learned behav-ior, is acquired through classical and operant conditioning, social learn-ing, discrimination, and generalization.

## Problem Solving Example:

Define behaviorism and social learning theory.

Behaviorism refers to a theory that considers only observable behavior. Behaviorists are not interested in mental processes that cannot be observed. B.F. Skinner, the major exponent of behavior-ist theory, believes that "emotions" are fictional causes of behavior. This school of thought only measures and analyzes behavior that can be seen – namely, stimuli and responses. Indeed, behaviorist theory is concerned solely with stimulus-response (S→R) behavior.

Behaviorism considers the environment an extremely important influence upon child development. While Skinner has no elaborate or systematic theory of child development, he does see it as a building process. Each new experience adds to a child's dimension and molds him into the person he will eventually become. This view comes as no surprise since behaviorists, with their emphasis on behavior modifica-tion and behavioral shaping, see the individual's environment as cru-cial to his development.

Social learning theory is based on the fact that children imitate. Social learning theory is purportedly related to behaviorism since both involve the principles of operant conditioning (the reinforcement of an unsolicited response). Children's unsolicited imitation is reinforced through various means in social learning theory, either by the child himself or others around him.

Some social learning theories include Freudian concepts. However, they do not include Freud's concepts of the unconscious and the basic instinctual drives.

Social learning theory is still being developed and modified. The major components of this theory include the importance of dependency as the major factor that brings about socialization, and aggression as an energy that is channeled into socially acceptable behavior as the child matures.

### 2.2.1  Skinner's Ideas

**B. F. Skinner** (1904 – 1990) and other traditional behaviorists believed that everything a person does is ultimately based on past and present rewards and punishments and other aspects of operant conditioning. He rejected the idea that personality is made up of consistent traits and denied that a personality or self initiates or directs behavior.

Skinner did not use the term personality. For Skinner, what other theorists call personality is nothing more than a collection of learned behaviors that have been reinforced in the past.

For Skinner, therefore, personality is a person's observed behaviors and does not contain internal traits or thoughts. Consistency in behavior occurs because of consistency in environmental experiences. Also, according to behaviorists, because personality is learned, it can be changed by rearranging experiences and situations.

## Problem Solving Example:

 What implications does the theorizing of B.F. Skinner and other behaviorists have for personality theory?

B.F. Skinner has contributed much to establishing the importance of operant conditioning in learning and in the application of its principles to personality development, psychopathology, educational problems and to other areas. In operant conditioning, the experimenter waits until the subject makes a desired response and then rewards him for the response.

This school of thought objects to the postulation of inner mechanisms as explanations for observable behaviors. Inner drives of any type whether they be unconscious ids or self-actualizing impulses are viewed as being equally irrelevant to explaining observed responses once the environmental stimuli controlling those responses are identified. Thus, from a behaviorist's point of view, postulating traits or inner drives is merely a redundant statement of the behavior that has already been observed and serves more to satisfy the fancy of the theorist than to advance the knowledge and understanding of human behavior.

Implicit in operant conditioning is that the environment is responsible for the formation of an individual's pattern of responses that can be labeled as his personality. Through appropriate environmental control then, healthy personalities could be programmed. It is, thus, necessary for behavioral scientists to focus on controlling the variables in the environment that act on the individual.

In the treatment of psychopathology, reward and punishment would be seen as the most appropriate means of altering the aberrant behavior of the patient. From this point of view, enough punishment administered for unhealthy behavior patterns would eventually serve to remove that behavior pattern and sufficient reward given for healthy behaviors will eventually make that behavior pattern a part of the individual's personality. Typically, rewarding desired behaviors has been proven to be more effective in eliciting desired behaviors than punishing unwanted actions.

## 2.2.2 Social Learning

The group of psychologists who emphasize behavior, environment, and cognition as important in determining personality are known as **social learning theorists** (sometimes referred to as **cognitive-behavioral** or **social-cognitive approach**).

Social learning theorists differ from the behavioral view of Skinner by emphasizing that we can regulate and control our own behavior despite changes in our environment.

**Albert Bandura**, **Walter Mischel**, and **Julian Rotter** are three social learning theorists.

**Bandura** believes that learning occurs by observing what others do and that these observations form an important part of our personality. Bandura suggested that how people behave in a variety of situations is determined by **self-efficacy** or their expectations of success. Those high in self-efficacy will approach new situations confidently and persist in their efforts because they believe success is likely. People low in self-efficacy expect to do poorly and avoid challenges.

According to Bandura, **reciprocal determinism** (sometimes called **reciprocal influences**) influences individual differences in personality. This means that personality, behavior, and environment constantly influence one another and shape each other in a reciprocal fashion.

# Problem Solving Example:

**Q** Describe social learning theory, as formulated by Bandura and Mischel.

**A** Social learning theory, first described by Miller and Dollard, is an attempt to combine the principles of social analysis of behavior with principles of learning taken from the behavior scientist's animal laboratory. Beginning with a criticism of certain aspects of Miller and Dollard's theory, Bandura and Mischel have developed their own social learning theory with the emphasis on the acquisition of responses through "modeling." Modeling consists of imitating the behavior of another person. For modeling behavior to occur, the individual must have the necessary skills to imitate the model and be motivated to do so.

When accompanied by positive reinforcement, imitation is an efficient technique for learning the social roles that are expected of a person in various situations. With an aggressive, fearful, suspicious, antisocial or hypochondriacal model, however, the individual will not learn socially useful behaviors. Thus, the quality of models is quite important in the development of psychologically healthy responses.

They emphasize that the whole range of learned behavior can be acquired and also modified through modeling or observational learning as it is also called. Observational learning involves four basic processes: attention to the model, retention of the relevant model cues, reproduction of the model's performance, and reinforcement. Reinforcement may be direct or vicarious. Learning can therefore take place merely by the imitator feeling the model's rewards and punishments and modifying his own behavior as a result. Subjects not only imitate their model's behavior, they also create new behaviors within the same context. For example, a child who sees an adult slapping a doll will not only slap it when it is given to him, he may also hit it with a bat.

The social learning theory of Bandura and Mischel has been applied to psychotherapy, modeled aggression and tests of competing theories of model-identification. The recent work has been carried on by Bandura after Mischel's death. Basing his work on established empirical laboratory principles, Bandura has worked to extend behavior theory beyond its stimulus-response-reinforcement early days. He has begun to encompass the less observable but more human aspect of people – their capacity to interpret and their awareness of themselves as interpreters of their lives.

According to **Mischel**, person variables as well as situation variables are important in explaining behavior. Mischel believes that behavior is characterized more by **situational specificity** than by consistency. That is, we often behave differently in different situations.

**Rotter** believed personality is determined by a person's **generalized expectations** about future outcomes and reinforcements. Rotter proposed that **locus of control** influences how we behave. Those with an **internal locus of control** see themselves primarily in control of their behavior and its consequences. Persons with an **external locus of control** see their behavior as controlled by fate, chance, or luck and are less likely to change their behavior as a result of reinforcement because they do not understand the relationship between the reinforcement and their behavior.

## Problem Solving Example:

Describe Rotter's Locus of Control scale and what it attempts to measure.

"Locus of control" as a determinant of individual behavior is predicated on the notion that an important underlying determinant of an individual's action is the degree to which an individual perceives that a reward follows from his own behavior or is controlled by forces outside himself. Lefcourt (1966) described the difference in these orientations: the person with an internal orientation tends to take responsibility for what happens to him, he sees the events of life as having a cause-effect relationship with himself as the cause; the external sees the events of life as due to chance or fate or some other factor beyond his control. The difference between people with regard to locus of control is one of degree and it is also situation dependent. In situations with which people have very little experience the generalized tendency measured by the locus of control scale will tend to have considerable effect.

The actual scale consists of twenty-six forced choice items, 13 of which indicate an external orientation* and 13 of which indicate an internal orientation. Examples from the scale are:

*a. Many of the unhappy things in people's lives are partly due to bad luck.

b. People's misfortunes result from the mistakes they make.

a. Promotions are earned through hard work and persistence.

*b. Making a lot of money is largely a matter of getting the right breaks.

The asterisked statements represent an external orientation. Items of this kind from the scale have been administered to a variety of different populations for research purposes. Quite consistent findings are found, some of which are: individuals with high achievement motivation are found to be more internal in their dispositions; males are routinely more internal than females; whites are more internal than blacks; internals are more resistant to influence attempts than externals.

As a part of a person's personality, locus of control is a learned or acquired characteristic and can therefore be changed by new experiences. It is also probably highly dependent on cultural values. In our culture an internal orientation is most highly valued, whereas in India, for instance, the culture would be more likely to favor and reinforce the external world view.

### 2.2.3 Evaluating the Behavioral Perspective

The main strengths of the behavior perspective are its strong research base and testability.

*Criticisms* of the behavioral perspective of personality include:

They do not consider possible unconscious motives or internal dispositions or traits that might be consistent from situation to situation.

There has been little effort to integrate possible biological factors or genetic influences into their theories of personality.

Historically, they have relied too much on animal research.

They have not paid attention to possible enduring qualities of personality.

They tend to be **reductionistic**, meaning they try to explain the complex concept of personality in terms of one or two factors.

They have focused more on environment and less on cognition.

## 2.3 The Trait Approach

The **trait** or **dispositional approaches** to personality focus on durable tendencies or dispositions to behave in a particular way in a variety of situations. According to trait theories, people can be described in terms of the basic ways that they behave, such as friendly, moody, dependable, etc.

While trait theorists sometimes disagree on which traits make up personality, they all agree that traits are the fundamental building blocks of personality. Trait theorists also debate how many dimensions are necessary to describe personality. Most trait approaches assume that some traits are more basic than others.

*Basic assumptions* of the trait approach to personality are:

1. Each person has **stable dispositions** to display certain behaviors, attitudes, and emotions.

2. These dispositions or traits are **general** and appear in **diverse situations**.

3. Each person has a **different set of traits**.

4. Trait theorists include Gordon Allport, Hans Eysenck, and Raymond Cattell.

### 2.3.1 Basic Five Traits

More recently, a number of studies have revealed five basic dimensions of personality. These are referred to as the **Big Five traits** or **factors** of personality.

There has been some disagreement about how to name these five traits. Three possible listings include:

**extroversion-introversion**

**friendly compliance versus hostile noncompliance**

**neuroticism**

**will to achieve**

**intellect**

or

**extroversion**

**agreeableness**

**conscientiousness**

**emotional stability**

**openness to experience**

or

**extroversion**

**neuroticism**

**agreeableness**

**openness to experience**

**conscientiousness**

## 2.3.2 Sheldon's Body Types

An American physician, **William Sheldon**, found a moderate correlation between body type or physique and personality.

| Body type (physique) | Personality |
|---|---|
| **Endomorph** | **Viscerotonic** |
| Soft, round, fairly weak muscles and bones | Relaxed, loves to eat, sociable |

| Mesomorph | Somatotonic |
|---|---|
| Muscular, athletic | Energetic, assertive, courageous |
| **Ectomorph** | **Cerebrotonic** |
| Thin, physically weak, sensitive nervous system | Restrained, fearful, introvert, artistic |

There is no research evidence, however, to validate the relationship between body type and personality, and Sheldon's theory is not considered to be valid today. Sheldon's model is better understood as a historic example of efforts to classify individuals according to personality traits.

## Problem Solving Example:

 Describe the system of somatotyping as proposed by Sheldon (1940).

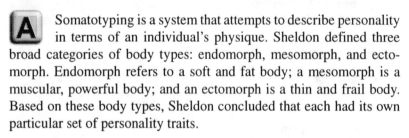 Somatotyping is a system that attempts to describe personality in terms of an individual's physique. Sheldon defined three broad categories of body types: endomorph, mesomorph, and ectomorph. Endomorph refers to a soft and fat body; a mesomorph is a muscular, powerful body; and an ectomorph is a thin and frail body. Based on these body types, Sheldon concluded that each had its own particular set of personality traits.

An endomorph is characterized by a temperament that is jolly, relaxed, friendly and easy-going. William Howard Taft and Santa Claus are classic examples of endomorphs. A mesomorphic individual is brave, bold, aggressive, and powerful. A number of professional athletes could be considered mesomorphic. An ectomorph is a shy, weak, delicate and socially withdrawn individual.

Most American psychologists ignore Sheldon's findings. Clearly, few people fit into any one particular category. Such a simplistic system is not often useful.

### 2.3.3 Evaluating the Trait Approach

There is evidence to support the view that there are internal traits that strongly influence behavior across situations and some traits appear stable over time.

*Criticisms* of the trait theory maintain:

Personality often does change according to a given situation.

Trait theorists do not attempt to explain why people have certain traits and it is, therefore, not a comprehensive approach to the study of personality.

Trait approach is more of a research technique than a theory.

The debate continues concerning what (and how many) traits are related to personality.

## Problem Solving Example:

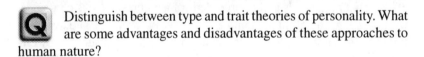

Distinguish between type and trait theories of personality. What are some advantages and disadvantages of these approaches to human nature?

Historically, the most common way of approaching personality has been in terms of traits. "Traits" are enduring and stable characteristics within an individual that provoke him to action in some consistent way. Trait psychology represented one of the earliest attempts to introduce order into the multiplicity of human behavior. It is a simple approach – as it looks for consistencies in behavior.

Examples of traits that have been studied are: extroversion-introversion (perhaps the most common studied), submissiveness-dominance, honesty-dishonesty, and intelligence. The dimension of extroversion-introversion was popularized in the writings of Carl Jung, a psychoanalyst. One major difficulty with such characterizations is that they omit a great deal of individual variation around major types, as well as mixtures that may occur. For example, an individual is likely, in reading a description of extroverted and introverted behavior, to find both within himself.

Another approach to personality which attempted to isolate particular predicting characteristics of behavior within an individual was type psychology. This approach to human behavior dates back to the writings of Hippocrates and Galen in ancient Greece. According to their temperament theory, individual personality types can be classified into four categories on the basis of the dominance of one of four body fluids or humors: the sanguine, the choleric, the melancholic and the phlegmatic type.

A more modern theorist, Alfred Adler, includes a typology in his personality theory which relates to this early temperament theory. Adler developed his scheme of personality types based on the degree of social interest and activity level in different personalities. His types were: (1) The ruling-dominant type (choleric) – this person is assertive, aggressive and active. He manipulates and masters the events and situations of his life. While he has a high activity level, his social interest is low. (2) The getting-leaning type (phlegmatic) – this type expects others to satisfy his needs and to provide for his interests. He is characterized by a low social interest and a low activity level. (3) The avoiding type (melancholic) – this person is inclined to achieve success by circumventing a problem or withdrawing from it. Mastery is achieved by avoiding defeat. He has a low social interest and a very low activity level. (4) The socially useful type (sanguine) – this personality type is said to be the most healthy of all. The socially useful person attacks problems head on, he is socially oriented and is prepared to cooperate with others to master the tasks of life.

The danger with both trait and type theories is that labels of the above kind can be misleading, especially because they tend to disregard situational variables – they ignore the relationship between a person and his environment. They focus exclusively on responses that are too broad. Therefore, their application for prediction is limited except in cases of extremes.

Research that has been conducted to test trait and type theories has shown that traits are not consistent from situation to situation. For example, individuals that were honest in one circumstance were found to be dishonest in another. By ingenious methods, Hartshorne studied a large number of children in a variety of conditions in which honesty or dishonesty could be observed. For example, in one condition they returned their test papers so the children could grade their own papers. Their actual responses were known; therefore, the researchers could determine what, if any, changes were made. While a few children were found who were consistently honest and a few that were consistently dishonest, most varied considerably depending upon the circumstances. The results clearly established that honesty was not a stable trait but varied across situations.

Another criticism of trait or type theory is that any trait attributed to a person by an observer, such as high aggressiveness, is more easily explained as a product of the observer's personal reactions or measuring instrument. This makes the study of traits and types useful to psychologists interested in assessing a person's values and attitudes. The average person is believed to judge others by assigning them traits. The existence of these traits in the person being observed is irrelevant; what are important are the traits the observer chooses to assign. The careful analysis of this attribution process aids the psychologist in studying the person's values and attitudes.

## 2.4   The Humanistic Approach

The **humanistic approach** (sometimes referred to as **phenomenological approach**) to personality is an **optimistic** response to the pessimism of psychodynamic theorists. Humanistic psychologists emphasize immediate **subjective experiences** that are unique to each of us.

The humanistic approach stresses each person's capacity for personal growth, positive growth, free will, and freedom to choose one's destiny.

### 2.4.1 Rogers' Person-Centered Approach

**Carl Rogers'** (1902–1987) **person-centered approach** emphasizes that people have different perceived realities, strive toward self-actualization, and should be given unconditional positive regard.

Rogers used the term **phenomenal field** to describe each person's total subjective experience of reality.

The **self-concept** (or **self-image**) is the core theme in Rogers' theory. Self-concept refers to individuals' overall perceptions of their abilities, behavior, and personality. He distinguished between the **real self** (the self we form as a result of our experiences) and the **ideal self** (who we really want to be).

Maladjustment results from a discrepancy between the real self and the ideal self. An **incongruent person** is one who has a distorted or inaccurate self-image.

Experiences that match the self-image are **symbolized** and admitted to consciousness.

The development of the self-concept depends on **self-evaluations** and **positive evaluations** shown by **others**. Anxiety and other problems result, therefore, because of **incongruence** between self-evaluations and the evaluations of others.

Others can help a person develop a more positive self-concept through **unconditional positive regard**. That is, by being accepting, positive, and loving without special conditions or strings attached and regardless of the person's behavior.

Rogers also felt we can help others develop their self-concept by being **empathetic** (sensitive and understanding) and **genuine** (open with our feelings and dropping our pretenses).

According to Rogers, **fully functioning persons** are those who live in harmony with their deepest feelings, impulses, and intuitions. Rogers used the term **self-actualization** to describe the tendency for humans to fulfill their true potential.

(Psychotherapy based on Rogers' theory is presented in chapter 6.)

# Problem Solving Examples:

 Describe and define the structure of personality according to Carl Rogers.

According to Carl Rogers, the structure of the personality is based on two constructs, the organism and the self. The organism is conceived to be the locus of experience; experience includes everything available to awareness and all that occurs within the organism. The phenomenal field is the totality of experience as perceived by the individual, therefore, it includes both conscious and unconscious experiences. In Rogers' terminology, conscious experiences are referred to as symbolized experiences; unconscious experiences are not symbolized. The phenomenal field is the individual's internal frame of reference; it is his subjective reality. For an individual to act realistically he must determine if his subjective reality, his symbolized experiences, is discrepant with objective reality, the world. If there is a discrepancy, the individual may behave unrealistically and thereby, detrimentally. An individual should strive to reduce the incongruence between subjective and objective realities.

The self is a portion of the phenomenal field. Thus, the self or self-concept refers to the organized and consistent set of perceptions that are self-referential, i.e., that refer to "I" or "me." It also includes the perceptions of the relationships between "I" or "me" and the rest of the world, including other people. This concept of self is usually referred to as a self-as-object definition as opposed to a self-as-process definition. Rogers defines the self as the person's attitudes and feelings about himself; it is not a concept of self in which the self governs behavior and controls adjustment. It is important to note that the distinction between self-as-object and self-as-process is not absolute; there is usually some overlap between the two. In addition to the self, there is an ideal self which represents what the individual aspires to be.

The importance of Rogers' distinction between the organism and the self emerges when the issue of congruence and incongruence is raised. Incongruence between the self as perceived and the actual experience of the organism results in the individual feeling threatened, anxious, and defensive; his thinking becomes rigid and constricted. An individual is considered mature, well-adjusted, and psychologically healthy when there is congruence between the actual experience of the organism and the self-image. An example of an incongruence is the existence of hostile feelings together with an individual's self-image of being a nice person. Usually, the result of such a conflict will be a denial of the hostility because it is incongruent with the self-image. The denial results in anxiety and defensiveness. The defensiveness may result in the projection of the hostility to a different target so that it is perceived as something external to the individual. The individual perceives hostility in the treatment he receives from others. Congruence and incongruence also manifest themselves between subjective reality (the phenomenal field) and external reality and between the perceived self and the ideal self. Incongruence between the perceived self and the ideal self results in dissatisfaction and frustration.

The structure of the personality as conceptualized by Rogers is a highly organized and unified system. Rogers rejects atomism and segmentation in favor of Gestalt theory. Briefly, Gestalt theorists emphasize the "holistic" nature of things in the world; the whole is greater than the sum of its parts. They believe that people perceive things in wholes, not in parts, segments, or atoms.

**Q** In a family where all male members have been doctors for generations, Peter decides to become an artist. Although his parents claim to love him, they are very upset over his choice. How would Rogers explain this attitude shown by Peter's parents?

**A** Carl Rogers can be counted among the "humanistic" psychologists. Humanistic psychology emphasizes man's capacity for goodness, creativity and freedom; it sees man as a spiritual, rational, autonomous being. Rogers came to understand that an individual's personality was conditioned by his interactions with significant others. The evaluations of his behavior by the adults in his world are assimilated by the child's self-structure. Many behaviors consistent with his parents' conception of what he should be will be praised; while behaviors that are inconsistent with what his parents perceive him to be will be punished or responded to with emotional rejection. Through this process the child learns to experience reality second-hand, as he begins to be guided by the safe feelings he receives when he is engaged in behavior that is acceptable to his parents. Experience is thus distorted in the service of maintaining positive regard from his parents. This positive feedback eventually contributes to a "self" image that comes to dictate what types of events an individual will permit to enter awareness and what types will be excluded. Threatening self-perceptions are excluded.

Through this dynamic we may be able to understand how Rogers would explain the attitude of disapproval shown by Peter's parents when they discover that he intends to become an artist rather than follow the family tradition of becoming a doctor. In their self-structure is apparently the idea that they love their son – perhaps even unconditionally. Also part of their self concept may contain the idea that for male members of their family to be of value they must be doctors, as this is the way that the other doctors in the family received positive regard. When they learn that their son is not going to be a doctor, they discover that it is difficult to experience feelings of acceptance and support for him because it is threatening to their own self-structure. These two perceptions – that they love their son and that to be of value an individual in the family must be a doctor – are incongruent and will need to be worked through, perhaps therapeutically, if a positive solution is to be found.

### 2.4.2 Maslow's Theory of Self-Actualization

**Abraham Maslow** (1908–1970) is another humanistic psychologist and is best known for his study of **self-actualization**. Maslow studied individuals who he believed were using their abilities to their full potential. He found that these self-actualizers were accurate in perceiving reality, comfortable with life, accepting of themselves and others, did not depend on external authority, were autonomous and independent, had a good sense of humor about themselves and others, and had frequent **peak experiences** (experiences of insight and deep meaning).

Maslow developed a **hierarchy of motives** or **hierarchy of needs** in which each lower need must be satisfied before the next level can be addressed. These needs occur in the following sequence: **physiological, safety, love and belongingness, esteem,** and finally, **self-actualization**. (Maslow's hierarchy of motives is described in further detail in chapter 4).

## 2.4.3 Evaluating the Humanistic Approach

The humanistic or phenomenological approach has been useful in developing several types of psychotherapy and in suggesting child-rearing and educational practices. Other strengths are its positive interpretation of human nature and its focus on the present and future.

*Criticisms* of the humanistic or phenomenological approach include:

This approach may be better at describing behavior than explaining behavior.

The studies to support this approach are often inadequate and unscientific.

It is too selfish in focus. Humanistic theorists focus on what is good for the self but often ignore what is good for the general welfare of others.

It is too optimistic. The belief that all humans are driven by a positive and innate growth potential may be naive and unrealistic.

# CHAPTER 3

# Assessing Intelligence and Personality

## 3.1 Developing Tests

Assessing intelligence and personality is a complex activity. **Assessment**, in general, is an information-gathering process that leads to decisions concerning classification, placement, and treatment. Tests, observations, and interviews are the most common procedures used in the assessment process. This chapter focuses on tests used to determine intelligence and personality.

A **psychological test** is an objective, standardized measure of a sample of behavior. Both intelligence and personality tests are considered psychological tests.

Any good psychological test must meet three criteria – it must be standardized, reliable, and valid.

### 3.1.1 Standardization

**Standardization** involves developing uniform procedures for administering and scoring a test and developing norms for the test.

**Uniform procedures** require that the testing environment, test directions, test items, and amount of time allowed be as similar as possible for all individuals who take the test.

**Norms** are established standards of performance for a test. Norms inform us about which scores are considered high, average, or low. Norms are determined by giving the test to a large group of people **representative** of the **population** for whom the test is intended. Future test-takers' scores are determined by comparing their scores with those from the **standardization sample** or group that determined the norms.

A **percentile score** indicates the percentage of people who scored below a score that one has attained. If you attain a percentile score of 75, for example, that means that you scored higher than 74% of the sample of people who provided the test norms.

## 3.1.2 Reliability

**Reliability** is a measure of the consistency of a person's test scores. A test's reliability can be measured in several ways:

**Test-retest reliability**    Giving the same individuals the same test on two different occasions. If the results are similar, then the test is considered to have good test-retest reliability.

**Split-half reliability**    Individuals take only one test, but the test items are divided into two halves and performance on each half is compared. If individuals performed about equally well on each half of the test, the test has good split-half reliability.

**Alternate-form reliability**    Two alternate forms of the test are administered on two different occasions. Test items on the two forms are similar but not identical. If each person's score is similar on the two tests, alternate-form reliability is high.

Correlation coefficients are sometimes used to represent reliability. A **correlation coefficient** is a numerical index that represents the degree of relationship between two variables.

### 3.1.3 Validity

A **valid test** is one that measures what it purports to measure.

Methods to measure validity include:

| | |
|---|---|
| **Content validity** | The test's ability to cover the complete range of material (or content) that it is supposed to measure. |
| **Criterion validity** | Compares test scores to actual performance on another direct and independent measure of what the test is supposed to measure. |
| **Predictive validity** | A form of criterion validity. How well a test score predicts an individual's performance at some time in the future. |
| **Face validity** | How well the test and test items appear to be relevant. |
| **Construct validity** | How well a test appears to represent a **theoretical or hypothetical construct** (abstract qualities). It is the extent to which scores on a test behave in accordance with a theory about the construct of interest. |

## Problem Solving Example:

 What is a psychological test? What are the steps that one should follow in designing a test?

A psychological test may be defined as a "sample of behavior." That is, a psychological test is designed to extract information about a person in the form of test responses in a short period of time. Test responses are viewed as samples of behavior and from these samples the examiner attempts to gain some insight into, to form a profile of, the subject. In the case of an intelligence test the examiner may obtain a score (IQ) for the subject and make predictions based on this information as to how well the subject will perform in relevant situations. If the subject's IQ is relatively high it is expected that he will behave quite "intelligently." The examiner's job is to make accurate generalizations about the subject's usual behavior on the basis of a small sample of behavior (the test results).

There are four basic steps in test construction which should be followed in constructing most tests. First of all, the examiner should identify and analyze the characteristics of the subject matter to determine what content should be tested. Often this is done in accordance with a specific theory pertaining to that subject matter. On a test that measures anxiety, a theory about anxiety may be used to derive test content. The second step is to construct items that represent a reasonable portion of the behavioral domain of interest. Intelligence tests should test each individual aspect of intelligence in proportion to its importance in the construct as a whole. This is why the IQ tests have "subtests"; verbal ability or mathematical ability alone will not be an adequate reflection of a person's intelligence. The third step is to assess the reliability and validity of the test. Content validity is built into the test; an analysis of the subject matter or content of the test was undertaken before the construction of test items. The examiner therefore, will seek to establish criterion-related validity. He will correlate the test with some objective criteria that is an appropriate measure of the trait or ability the test is supposed to be measuring. If the test is either invalid or unreliable or both, the test must be revised. The fourth and final step is to formulate a strategy for making decisions about people based on test scores. That is, the examiner decides how he will go about generalizing profiles of individuals based on their test scores.

## 3.2   Intelligence Testing

**Aptitude tests** attempt to measure a person's capability for mastering an area of knowledge. (For instance, what is your potential or aptitude for learning a foreign language?)

**Achievement tests** assess the amount of knowledge someone has already acquired in a specific area (such as math achievement, reading achievement, etc.).

## Problem Solving Example:

 What is the distinction between an aptitude test and an achievement test?

It is not true that achievement tests measure solely the effects of learning and that aptitude tests measure solely "innate capacity" independent of learning. The distinction between aptitude and achievement tests is not absolute; it is a loose distinction.

Examiners usually apply the term aptitude to tests that measure the effects of learning under uncontrolled or unknown conditions. Moreover, the people who are taking aptitude tests have not usually undergone a uniform prior experience as have people who are taking "achievement tests." An example of a uniform prior experience is a geometry class; the New York State Regents Examination in geometry is an achievement test given to all who have undergone the uniform prior experience of taking a geometry class in a New York State public high school. The Scholastic Aptitude Tests' (SAT) math section is a math aptitude test because it is administered to students nationwide with a variety of unknown mathematical backgrounds.

The respective uses of achievement and aptitude tests are also different. Aptitude tests serve to predict subsequent performance, e.g., to determine if an individual will profit from the education at a particular college, if someone will perform well in a particular training program, etc. Achievement tests, on the other hand, are usually administered after training in order to evaluate what the individual has gained through training.

Since achievement tests and aptitude tests have different uses, they are usually validated in different ways. It is most appropriate to use content validity to assess an achievement test because having content validity assures that the test will be measuring an adequate and representative sample of the material covered during training. Criterion-related validity is used to determine if a test will accurately reflect future performance. Therefore, aptitude tests are assessed by criterion-related validity; that is, the test results are checked with a future measure of the same behavior which the test is designed to measure. For example, the SAT is designed to predict college performance; therefore, SAT scores are checked against college grades to make sure that high SAT scores mean that an individual will probably have high college grades.

It must be remembered, however, that the distinctions between achievement and aptitude tests are not strict. Achievement tests can be used to predict performance. The College Board's (CEEB) Achievement Tests in specific subjects, physics, for example, will predict an individual's future performance in college physics with some degree of accuracy, even though the test was not designed to predict future performance but past achievement.

Because intelligence is a **hypothetical construct**, psychologists have disagreed on how to define it. Different intelligence tests, therefore, ask different questions and may measure different abilities.

Some definitions of intelligence include:

- The capacity to acquire and use knowledge.
- The total body of acquired knowledge.
- The ability to arrive at innovative solutions to problems.
- The ability to deal effectively with one's environment.
- Knowledge of one's culture.
- The ability to do well in school.
- It is the global capacity of the individual to act purposefully, to think rationally, and to deal effectively with the environment.
- Intelligence is what intelligence tests measure.

A major question related to intelligence has been "does intelligence consist of a single core factor or does it consist of many separate, unrelated abilities?" Responses to this include:

**Charles Spearman**

Concluded that cognitive abilities could be narrowed down to one critical **g-factor** or general intelligence. (The **s-factors** represent specific knowledge needed to answer questions on a particular test.)

**J. P. Guilford**

Proposed that intelligence consists of 180 distinct abilities.

**L. L. Thurstone**

Used a statistical technique known as **factor analysis** to find seven independent primary mental abilities: numerical ability, reasoning, verbal fluency, spatial visualization, perceptual ability, memory, and verbal comprehension.

**Raymond B. Cattell**

Argued that a g-factor does exist, but it consists of **fluid intelligence** (reasoning and problem solving) and **crystallized intelligence** (specific knowledge gained from applying fluid intelligence).

**Robert Sternberg**

Proposed a **triarchic theory of intelligence** that specifies three important parts of intelligence: **componential intelligence** (includes metacomponents, performance components, and knowledge-acquisition components), **experiential intelligence** (abilities to deal with novelty and to automatize processing), and **contextual intelligence** (practical intelligence and social intelligence).

**Howard Gardner**

**Theory of multiple intelligences** proposed seven different components of intelligence that include not only language ability, logical-mathematical thinking, and spatial thinking but also musical, bodily kinesthetic, interpersonal, and intra-personal thinking.

## 3.2.1  History of Intelligence Testing

Early interest in intelligence testing dates back to the **eugenics movement** of **Sir Frances Galton**. Galton believed that it is possible to improve genetic characteristics (including intelligence) through breeding.

The first effective test of intelligence was devised in the early 1900s by French psychologist **Alfred Binet**. Binet was appointed by the French Ministry of Public Instruction to design an intelligence test that would identify children who needed to be removed from the regular class-rooms so that they could receive special instruction.

Binet and his colleague **Theodore Simon** devised an intelligence test consisting of 30 subtests containing problems of increasing diffi-culty. The items on the test were designed to measure children's judg-ment, reasoning, and comprehension. This first test was published in 1905 and then revised in 1908 and 1911.

The 1908 revision of the Binet and Simon scale introduced the notion of **mental age**. Mental age is a measure of a child's intellectual level that is independent of the child's **chronological age** (actual age).

Shortly after Binet's original work, **Lewis M. Terman** of Stanford University and his colleagues helped refine and standardize the test for American children. Their version came to be the **Stanford-Binet In-telligence Scale**, and its latest revision is still being used today. (A further discussion of this scale can be found later in this chapter.)

Terman and others (e.g., **L. William Stern** of Germany) devel-oped the idea of the **IQ** or **intelligence quotient** (sometimes referred to as **ratio IQ score**).

To **calculate IQ**, a child's **mental age (MA)** (as determined by how well she/he does on the test) is **divided by** her/his **chronological age (CA)** and **multiplied by 100**. That is,

$$IQ = \frac{MA}{CA} \times 100$$

The major advantage of the IQ score over simple MA is that it gives an index of a child's IQ test performance relative to others of the same chronological age.

The major problem with the ratio IQ score is that most people's mental development slows in their late teens. But as MA may remain fairly stable throughout adulthood, CA increases over time. Using CA as the divisor in the IQ formula, therefore, results in an individual's IQ score diminishing over time (even though MA has not changed).

**David Wechsler** corrected this problem with ratio IQ scores by devising the **deviation IQ score**. This deviation IQ score is calculated by converting the raw scores on each subtest of the test to **standard scores** normalized for each age group. These standard scores are then translated into deviation IQ scores.

Wechsler reasoned that intelligence is **normally distributed** or follows the bell-shaped curve – that is, the majority of people score at or around the **mean** or average score of 100 and progressively fewer people will achieve scores that spread out in either direction of the mean. A group of IQ scores can be portrayed as a normal, bell-shaped curve with an average score of 100 and a **standard deviation** (average deviation from the mean) that is the same (i.e., 15) at every age level. The figure on the next page presents the normal distribution of intelligence scores.

The advantage of the deviation IQ is that the standing of an individual can be compared with the scores of others of the same age, and the intervals from age to age remain the same. **Deviation IQ scores**, therefore, indicate exactly where a test-taker falls in the normal distribution of intelligence.

Terman adopted the deviation IQ as the scoring standard for the 1960 revision of the Stanford-Binet Intelligence Scale, although he

## Normal Distribution of Intelligence
(Based on tests with a standard deviation of 15)

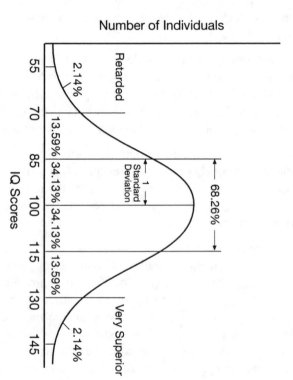

Number of Individuals

Retarded

2.14%

13.59% | 34.13% | 34.13% | 13.59%

1 Standard Deviation

68.26%

Very Superior

2.14%

55　70　85　100　115　130　145

IQ Scores

Approximately two-thirds of the IQ scores of any age group fall within one standard deviation above and below the mean score of 100. Notice that extremely high and extremely low scores are rare.

chose a standard deviation of 16 rather than 15. Almost all other intelligence tests today use deviation IQ scores.

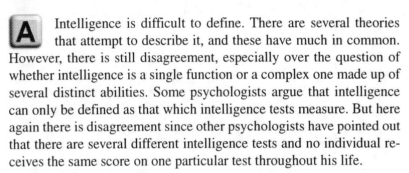

## Problem Solving Example:

**Q** Describe IQ. What is an IQ supposed to indicate? Trace the development of the IQ test from its beginnings.

**A** Intelligence is difficult to define. There are several theories that attempt to describe it, and these have much in common. However, there is still disagreement, especially over the question of whether intelligence is a single function or a complex one made up of several distinct abilities. Some psychologists argue that intelligence can only be defined as that which intelligence tests measure. But here again there is disagreement since other psychologists have pointed out that there are several different intelligence tests and no individual receives the same score on one particular test throughout his life.

IQ stands for intelligence quotient, and this has long been assumed to provide a reliable index for determining one's mental ability. The first attempt to measure IQ was in 1905 when the French psychologists Alfred Binet and Theodore Simon devised what has come to be called the Binet-Simon Scale. The scale consisted of a list of questions that became increasingly difficult as the list went on. School children were asked to answer the questions in order and the point at which they could no longer answer determined their mental age. The use of this test became widespread and several countries adopted it.

When Lewis M. Terman at Stanford University adapted the test for use in the United States, he rewrote large portions of it. In addition, he revised the method for expressing the test's results. By dividing the individual's test age or mental age by his actual age and multiplying this number by 100 (in order to avoid decimal fractions), he arrived at that person's IQ. Hence, Terman took into account the individual's intelligence in relation to others his own age. This new test became known as the Stanford-Binet test and was published in 1916. Since that time, it has been the most widely used of all intelligence tests.

A "normal" IQ is considered to be about 100, and 98 percent of the people who take this test fall in the range between 60 and 140. A person who scores below 60 is considered mentally challenged or disabled. Someone who scores above 140 is considered a "genius."

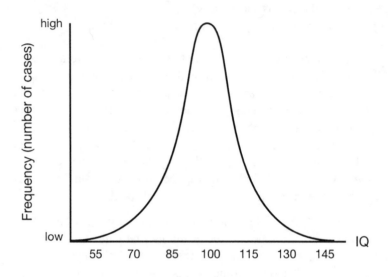

**The Normal Distribution of IQ Scores**

There have been several refinements on the Stanford-Binet test since its inception. One is the addition of performance portions in which the individual is asked to perform a certain task. This is included to enable infants and preschoolers who cannot read or write to take the test. Refinements have also been made in the statistical procedures used to determine test results. Testing adult intelligence has also been a problem, since intelligence appears to stop developing after about age 16. The Stanford-Binet test allowed for this by using 16 as a cutoff age; in other words, anyone 16 years or older is considered to be 16.

The Stanford-Binet test has stimulated heated criticism and debate. Some argue that IQ only indicates that person's performance ability on taking the test. However, it has been found that IQ tests do have some value in that they can predict how well an individual may do in school and in some jobs, for example. But because intelligence is so complex and related to so many other factors, one should be wary of depending too much on a single score as an indicator of success or failure.

### 3.2.2 Current Intelligence Tests

The two most widely used versions of intelligence tests today are described next. These tests are **individually administered**, which means that they are given only by trained psychologists to one test-taker at a time.

The first **Stanford-Binet Intelligence Scale** was published in 1916 by **Lewis Terman** and his colleagues. It was revised in 1937, 1960, and 1986 and remains one of the world's most widely used tests of intelligence (although there are criticisms of the scale). It can be used with individuals from age two through adulthood.

In its latest revision, Stanford-Binet Intelligence Scale: Fourth Edition, the term intelligence has been replaced by cognitive development. The terms intelligence, IQ, and mental age are not used; instead the term **Standard Age Score (SAS)** is used. The fourth edition measures four areas of cognitive development and a SAS can be calculated for each area as well as an overall composite score. The four areas measured are called Verbal Reasoning, Abstract/Visual Reasoning, Quantitative Reasoning, and Short-Term Memory.

Because the Stanford-Binet initially appeared to be unsatisfactory for use with adults, in 1939 David Wechsler published a test designed exclusively for adults. This test has since been revised several times and is now known at the **WAIS-III** or **Wechsler Adult Intelligence Scale, Third Edition**.

Eventually, Wechsler published two scales for children and these are now known as:

**WPPSI-R**　　　**Wechsler Preschool and Primary Scale of Intelligence, Revised** (for children 4 to 6 years of age)

**WISC-III**　　　**Wechsler Intelligence Scale for Children, 3rd edition** (for children 6 to 16 years of age)

The Wechsler scales were known for at least two major innovations when they were first developed. First, they were less dependent on verbal ability than the Stanford-Binet and included many items that required nonverbal reasoning. His tests allow the computation of three scores, a **Verbal IQ score**, a **Performance IQ score**, and an overall **Full Scale IQ score**. For example, subtests from the verbal and performance sections of the **WAIS-III** include:

| Verbal Subtests | Performance Subtests |
| --- | --- |
| Information | Digit Symbol |
| Comprehension | Picture Completion |
| Arithmetic | Block Design |
| Similarities | Picture Arrangement |
| Digit Span | Matrix Reasoning |
| Vocabulary | Symbol Search |
| Letter-Number Sequencing | |

Second, Wechsler developed the **deviation IQ score** based on the normal distribution of intelligence and abandoned the notion of intelligence quotient.

Wechsler's scales of intelligence are still widely used and respected today.

Intelligence tests, as with any other test, must fit certain requirements in order to be of good quality.

*Reliability.* Most intelligence tests used today (e.g., Stanford-Binet and Wechsler scales) demonstrate good reliability or consistency of scores.

*Validity.* The validity of intelligence tests depends on the criterion being used. For example, they do a good job of predicting success in school. Although intelligence test scores correlate with occupational attainment, they do not predict performance within a given occupation.

*Stability.* Intelligence test scores can and do change over time. For instance, infant and preschool scores are not good predictors of intelligence in later childhood, adolescence, or adulthood. It is not until late elementary school (e.g., after age 8 – 10) that intelligence test scores begin to stabilize. It is also possible, however, to make substantial gains or losses in intelligence during adolescence and adulthood.

## Problem Solving Examples:

 What are the Wechsler Intelligence Scale for Children (WISC) and the Wechsler Preschool and Primary Scale of Intelligence?

Both the Wechsler Intelligence Scale for Children (WISC) and the Wechsler Preschool and Primary Scale of Intelligence (WPPSI) are adaptations of the Wechsler Adult Intelligence Scale (WAIS). The WISC is normally administered to children from the ages of 6 1/2-16 1/2 and the WPPSI is normally administered to children from the ages of 4-6 1/2 years. Both the WISC and the WPPSI are divided into subtests for the purpose of easy evaluation of specific problems.

The WISC-III subtests are the same as the WAIS-III subtests, except for a few noted differences. The WISC-III includes two subtests, mazes and object assembly, that are not included on the adult version. Mazes consist of nine paper-and-pencil mazes of increasing difficulty, each to be completed in a set time. Object Assembly involves putting together puzzle pieces to make specific shapes. The WAIS-III includes two subtests, Letter-Number Sequencing and Matrix Reasoning, that are not on the WISC-III. Letter-Number Sequencing involves simultaneously remembering and arranging in order various numbers and letters. Matrix Reasoning involves solving nonverbal logic problems.

The WPPSI-R subtests differ somewhat from the WAIS-III subtests. There is no Digit Span or Letter-Number Sequencing subtest but sometimes a Sentences subtest is given as a supplementary test. On the Sentences subtest, the child is asked to immediately repeat a sentence orally presented to him by the examiner; thus, the Sentences subtest also serves as a memory test similar to the Digit Span subtest.

The performance scale substitutes the Animal House subtest for the Coding test. The child is given a key which pairs an animal with a colored cylinder which is referred to as the animal's house. The child is to insert the correctly colored cylinder in the hole beneath each animal on the board. The Geometric Design test requires the copying of 10 simple designs with a colored pencil. The Picture Arrangement Matrix Reasoning and Coding subtests from the WAIS-III are eliminated. The Mazes and Object Assembly subtest of the WISC are permanently included.

There were special efforts made to eliminate items from the WISC-III and the WPPSI-R that would be unfamiliar to certain groups of children; moreover, there were more female and black subjects in the pictorial content of the subtests. Thus, some attempt was made to eliminate the cultural bias of the test.

As in the WAIS-III, the subtests of the WISC-III and WPPSI-R can be scored separately for the purpose of identifying individual problem areas. The subtest scores are added and then converted to deviation IQ's with a mean of 100 and a standard deviation of 15. The reliability coefficients for both the WISC-III and the WPPSI-R are very high.

 What is the Stanford-Binet Intelligence Scale?

The Stanford-Binet Intelligence Scale is a substantially revised version of an intelligence test first constructed by Alfred Binet in 1905. Binet's original test, constructed for the purpose of separating intellectually normal children from intellectually subnormal children, was first revised by Terman, a psychologist from Stanford University, in 1916 (thus the name Stanford-Binet). In 1937, two parallel forms of the Stanford-Binet test were constructed; the best items of these two forms were combined in order to construct the 1960 revision of the

Stanford-Binet. The currently used version, The Standford-Binet Intelligence Scale: Fourth Edition, was published in 1986.

The Stanford-Binet test is individually administered by a trained examiner. In total, there are fifteen subtests chosen to tap into four major cognitive areas: verbal reasoning, abstract/visual reasoning, quantitative reasoning, and short-term memory. The individual subtests are administered in a mixed sequence in order to keep up attention and interest for the test taker. The difficulty range of six of the tests spans the entire age range of the scale. Because of the nature of the tasks, the remaining nine tests either begin at a higher level or end at a lower level.

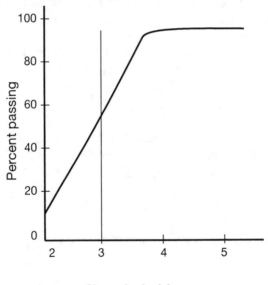

**Chronological Age**

Most children of average intelligence at a given age will pass an item designed for that age group.

The method of scoring the Stanford-Binet test is complicated. First, the examiner determines the child's basal age. Basal age is reached when four items on two consecutive levels are passed. Testing is then continued until the level is reached at three out of four or all four items on two consecutive levels are failed; this is called the ceiling age.

The Stanford-Binet test is well-known for its high reliability and its high predictive value. The Stanford-Binet is very accurate in the prediction of future academic achievement and thus it may be best thought of as largely a measure of scholastic aptitude or achievement and not of intelligence per se.

### 3.2.3   Extremes of Intelligence

Two basic extremes of intellectual performance are demonstrated on the extreme left and right of the normal distribution for intelligence.

In order to be considered **mentally retarded**, an individual must meet all three of the essential features described below:

1.   Intellectual functioning must be **significantly below average**. Today intelligence test scores of below 70 – or 2 standard deviations below the mean – are considered significantly below average.

2.   Significant deficits in **adaptive functioning** must be evident. Adaptive functioning refers to social competence or independent behavior that is expected based on chronological age.

3.   Onset must be **prior** to **age 18**.

Four general categories or ways of classifying mental retardation include:

| Category | Percentage | IQ Range | Characteristics |
|----------|-----------|----------|-----------------|
| **Mild** | 85% | 50 – 70 | May complete 6th grade academic work; may learn vocational skills and hold a job; may live independently as an adult. |

| Moderate | 10% | 35 – 49 | May complete 2nd grade academic work; can learn social and occupational skills; may hold job in sheltered workshop. |
|----------|-----|---------|------|
| Severe | 3 – 4% | 35 – 49 | May learn to talk or communicate; through repetition may learn basic health habits; often needs help for simple tasks. |
| Profound | 1% | less than 20 | Little or no speech; may learn limited self-help skills; requires constant help and supervision. |

There are hundreds of known causes of mental retardation. Many of them are biological, genetic, chromosomal, prenatal, perinatal, and postnatal in origin. Mental retardation can also result from environmental influences such as sensory or maternal deprivation. In some cases (especially mild mental retardation), the cause of an individual child's mental retardation is unknown.

**Giftedness** is often defined as having an intelligence of 120 to 130 or higher (or having an IQ in the upper 2 to 3 percent of the population).

**Lewis Terman** began a **longitudinal study** of gifted children in the 1920s. That is, he and others followed the lives of these children as they grew up and became adults. The study will not be completed until the year 2010. The average intelligence score was 150 for the approximately 1,500 children in this study. The findings of this study have challenged the commonly held belief that the intellectually gifted are emotionally disturbed and socially maladjusted. In fact, just the opposite was found. As adults, this group was also more academically and professionally successful than their non-gifted peers.

**Creativity** is the ability to think about something in novel and unusual ways and to come up with unique solutions to problems.

Creativity usually involves **divergent thinking** or the ability to generate many different but plausible responses to a problem.

Creative individuals tend to be more independent, rely more on intuitive thinking, have a higher degree of self-acceptance, and have more energy. Personality disorders are not more common among creative individuals.

There is not a very high correlation between intelligence and creativity. This is because most intelligence tests measure **convergent thinking** (producing one correct answer) and do not measure divergent thinking.

### 3.2.4   Determinants of Intelligence

The **nature vs. nurture debate** related to intelligence addresses whether heredity or environment determines one's intellectual skills.

**Heritability** is an estimate of how much of a trait in a population is determined by genetic inheritance.

In the late 1960s, **Arthur Jensen** argued that intelligence is approximately 80% due to heredity. He felt that the difference in mean intelligence scores for different races, nationalities, and social classes was due more to heredity than to environment.

Correlational studies with twins suggest that heredity influences the development of intelligence. For instance, the correlation of intelligence test scores for identical twins (who have identical genetic makeup) is higher than the correlation for fraternal twins. Even identical twins reared apart have more similar IQs than fraternal twins reared together in the same household.

There is research evidence, however, to indicate that environment also exerts a strong influence on intelligence. **Sandra Scarr** and other researchers have shown that underprivileged children placed in homes that provide an enriching intellectual environment have shown moderate but consistent increases in intelligence. Children placed in various enrichment programs have also shown gains in IQ. The IQs of identical twins reared together in the same environment are more similar than those for identical twins reared apart.

The term **reaction range** has been applied to the nature vs. nurture debate of intelligence. **Reaction range** implies that genetics may limit or define a potential range of IQ but that environment can influence where along this range an individual's IQ score falls. For instance, children in an enriched environment should score near the top of their potential IQ range.

Racial and cultural differences in IQ are very small when compared to the range of genetic differences within each group. Research has suggested, for example, that the differences between mean intelligence test scores for black and white Americans may be due to differences in parental education, nutrition, health care, schools, and motivation for doing well on the test.

Many have argued that intelligence tests are **culturally biased** because they have been developed by white, middle-class psychologists. There is some research evidence to support this claim. Attempts have been made to produce language-free, culture-fair tests of intelligence. The **Raven's Progressive Matrices** is one such test.

## Problem Solving Examples:

Discuss the influence of heredity on intelligence. Cite the hypotheses of Jensen and Bronfenbrenner.

### Correlations Between IQ Scores for Persons with Varying Degrees of Genetic Similarity

| | |
|---|---|
| Identical twins reared together | .87 |
| Identical twins reared apart | .75 |
| Fraternal twins reared together | .53 |
| Siblings reared together | .55 |

| | |
|---|---|
| Parents and their children | .50 |
| First cousins | .26 |
| Grandparent-grandchild | .27 |
| Unrelated children reared together | .23 |
| Unrelated children reared apart | .00 |

**A** Several studies have indicated that heredity plays a major role in determining intelligence. Hunt (1961), for example, found that the average correlation coefficient of intelligence test scores for identical twins is about .90. (For fraternal twins it is about .65). The study showed that as genetic similarity among individuals decreased, so did the similarity between intelligence test scores. Hence, identical twins had the highest correlation between test scores, while unrelated children had the lowest (.00). The correlations between the test scores in siblings was estimated at .50. Hunt's results clearly support a genetic influence.

Other studies involving twins also show heredity to be a major influence on intelligence. Muller (1925) found that identical twins showed negligible differences in intelligence test scores, even after they had been raised in different environments ("split-twin" studies). In a classic case involving identical twins, Jessie and Bessie, Muller found that Bessie, who grew up in a relatively poor family and had only four year of school, scored two points higher on an IQ test than Jessie, who grew up in an affluent family and had completed high school.

Newman, Freeman, and Holzinger (1937) substantiated Muller's findings. They found that monozygotic twins who were raised in dissimilar environments obtained intelligence tests scores which were more similar than were the scores of dizygotic (fraternal) twins who grew up together.

Arthur Jensen (1969) advanced a controversial theory which holds that heredity is most responsible for an individual's intelligence level. He estimated that the contribution of heredity to intelligence is 80 percent while the environment's contribution is only 20 percent. This estimate was derived from comparisons of intelligence test scores among different racial groups. Jensen found that African Americans did not perform as well as American Caucasians and that Caucasians did not perform as well as Asians. Jensen argues that the most important environmental influences on intelligence are prenatal; however, differences in test scores between those of different racial and social classes cannot be attributed to environment alone. This conclusion invites racist interpretations and has been hotly debated. According to Jensen's 80-20 ratio of the influence of heredity and environment, it would follow that American Caucasians have more potential for intellectual activities than African Americans. Jensen also argued that compensatory educational programs are useless.

Urie Bronfenbrenner (1972) has questioned Jensen's 80-20 ratio. He suggests that the twin studies upon which Jensen bases his claims involved too many uncontrolled variables. For example, when Jensen studied the intelligence comparison of monozygotic twins who were raised in different environments, the cultural aspects were really quite similar.

Newman, Freeman, and Holzinger (1937) had previously reached an estimate of 50 percent for the amount of genetic influence on heredity. Later on, Fehr (1969) also found a 50 percent or less genetic influence on intelligence.

**Q** What are some of the characteristics of cross-cultural tests? Name four examples of popularly administered cross-cultural tests.

**A** Traditionally, cross-cultural tests have tried to eliminate those factors or characteristics not of interest that differentiate between two cultures. One example of such a characteristic is language. We may presume that the administrator of the test knows that the two cultures have different languages. Language differences are not of interest; the examiner is trying to measure some other variable (intelligence, perhaps). The examiner's concern, then, is that he wants to make sure that language does not affect his measure of intelligence.

There are two ways to deal with the problem of language. The first way is to translate a given test into the language of the target population. Translated tests have two problems, however. First, the translation may not be equivalent to the original. Second, the translated tests should be standardized on a new sample of speakers of that language. The second way to deal with the problem of language is to completely eliminate language from the test.

When educational backgrounds differ widely and perhaps some groups of examiners are inferior in reading skills it is best to eliminate reading and other verbal skills from the test.

Different cultures often differ with regard to the value attached to speed of performance; in some cultures the tempo of daily life is slower and there is less concern with accomplishing tasks as quickly as possible. These cultural differences may be attributable to climate differences or perhaps to differences between urban and rural environments. Therefore, cross-cultural tests often try to eliminate the influence of speed by allowing long time limits and putting no premium on faster performance.

The most important factor that cross-cultural tests differ on is test content. Certain tests may require that the examinee be familiar with the function of objects that are absent in his culture or that have different uses or values in his culture. Persons reared in certain cultures lack the experience to respond correctly to these items. Therefore, examiners who are interested in developing cross-cultural tests are careful about the nature of the test content.

The Leiter International Performance Scale is an individually administered performance scale that almost completely eliminates instructions, both spoken and pantomime. The examiner's comprehension of his task is considered as part of the test. The Leiter scale consists of a response frame with an adjustable card holder. The examiner administers the test by sliding a particular card with printed pictures on it onto the response frame. The examinee is given a set of blocks with printed pictures on them and is supposed to choose the blocks with the proper response pictures and insert them into the correct frame. Among the tasks included in the Leiter scale are: matching identical colors, shades of gray, forms, or pictures; copying a block design; picture completion, number estimation, analogies, series completion, recognition of age differences, spatial relations, footprint recognition, similarities, memory for a series, and classification of animals according to habitat. The Leiter Scale has no time limit. The scale is scored in terms of the ratio of mental age (MA) over chronological age.

$$\frac{\text{mental age}}{\text{chronological age}}$$

However, it should be noted that the Leiter Scale IQ does not always correlate highly with the Stanford-Binet and the Wechsler IQ's; it is probable that the Leiter IQ is a measure of different intellectual characteristics.

R. B. Cattell developed the Culture Fair Intelligence Test, a paper-and-pencil test available in three levels, each level having a varying number of subtests. The highest level consists of the following four subtests: series, classification, matrices, and conditions. For the series subtest, the examinee selects the item that completes the series. In classification, the examinee marks the item in each row that does not belong. The matrices subtest requires that the subject mark the item that completes the given matrix, or pattern. The subject's task in the conditions subtest is to insert a dot in one of the alternative designs so as to meet the same conditions indicated in the sample design. Unfortunately, Cattell's Culture Fair Intelligence Test does not completely compensate for cultural disadvantages. In cultures different from the one in which the test was developed, performance was considerably below the original norms. Moreover, African-American children of low socioeconomic level did no better on this test than on the Stanford-Binet.

The "Progressive Matrices" were developed by Raven and were designed to measure Spearman's "g" factor, i.e., innate generalized intellectual ability. The test consists of 60 matrices (designs), of varying complexity, from which a part has been removed. The subject's task is to choose the missing insert from a set of eight alternatives. The matrices are grouped in five series. The earlier series require accuracy of discrimination; the later, more difficult series involve analogies, permutation and alternation of pattern, and other logical relations. The test is only moderately successful in predicting future academic achievement. Studies in a number of non-European cultures have shown that the test is probably not suitable for groups with very dissimilar backgrounds.

In the Goodenough Draw-a-Man Test the subject (the test is designed for use with children) is simply instructed to "make a picture of a man; make the very best picture that you can." Emphasis is placed on the child's accuracy of observation and on the development of conceptual thinking, rather than on artistic skill. Credit is given for the inclusion of individual body parts, clothing details, proportion, perspective, and similar features. A total of 73 scorable items were selected on the basis of age differentiation, relation to total scores on the test, and relation to group intelligence test scores. Test scores are translated into standard scores with a mean of 100. Again, these test scores should not be confused with IQ. Unfortunately, it has been found that performance on this test is more dependent on differences in cultural background than was originally assumed. The search for a perfectly "culture-free test" is probably futile. It may be impossible to create a test free of all of the possible biasing variables.

What are the advantages and disadvantages of cross-cultural tests?

Recently, there has been much concern about the fairness of applying available intelligence tests to culturally disadvantaged groups. Culturally disadvantaged means that an individual is not assimilated into or knowledgeable about the culture he is living in. He often comes from another, different culture or is segregated from those cultural groups that dominate the society as a whole. It seems unfair to judge these individuals on the basis of their performances on tests that are inherently "culturally biased." There appears to be no question that IQ tests, achievement tests, and aptitude tests are culturally biased. The mere fact that one needs to be fairly proficient in English language skills to do well on these tests is evidence of cultural bias.

Thus, the advantage of developing cross-cultural tests is that it is possible to compensate for the disadvantages many individuals have been subjected to and to measure innate abilities, including general intellectual ability. In this way it is possible to compare people from different cultures fairly on the basis of innate ability.

The disadvantage of cross-cultural tests is that the predictive and diagnostic value of the intelligence test is often lost. The most valuable characteristic of the IQ test, especially the Stanford-Binet, is its ability to predict accurately an individual's future academic achievement. There is little gained by administering culture-fair tests if they do not provide useful information. Educators are primarily interested in using IQ tests to identify those students who will have difficulty succeeding within the system, i.e., within the culture. A poor score on an IQ test suggests that an individual may need special assistance if he is to succeed within the culture. Notice that this says little about innate intelligence. The culturally biased information is in a very real sense necessary information for succeeding within the culture. IQ tests, especially the Wechsler series, can also help to pinpoint specific problem areas for individuals. Culture-fair tests may be able to measure some innate ability but this measure is useless in a society where success is dependent on cultural assimilation and knowledge.

Thus, the problem is not with IQ tests per se; the problem is with their interpretation. IQ test scores should not be interpreted as being indicative of inherent, unchangeable intellectual differences. IQ scores do predict success within the society. They can, however, be increased in disadvantaged children by intervention programs.

## 3.3 Personality Testing

Psychologists use **personality tests** for four different purposes:

1. to aid in the diagnosis of psychological disorders,
2. to counsel people,
3. to select employees,
4. to conduct research.

There are three major categories of personality tests: self-report inventories, projective tests, and behavioral assessment.

### 3.3.1 Self-Report Inventories

**Self-report inventories** instruct people to answer questions about themselves – about their characteristic behaviors, beliefs, and feelings.

The most widely used self-report inventory is the **MMPI** or **Minnesota Multiphasic Personality Inventory**. The MMPI has been revised and is now known as the **MMPI-2**.

The MMPI was originally designed to aid in the diagnosis of psychological disorders. It measures aspects of personality that, when manifested to an extreme degree, are thought to be symptoms of disorders.

The MMPI-2 consists of 567 statements that require a "true," "false," or "cannot say" response. Sample statements include:

"People are out to get me."

"I smile at everyone I meet."

"I know who is responsible for my troubles."

The MMPI-2 yields scores on 14 subscales – 4 validity scales and 10 clinical scales.

The **validity scales** are used to determine if an individual has been careless or deceptive in taking the test. The validity scales include:

**Cannot say scale**

**Lie scale**

**Infrequency scale**

**Subtle defensiveness scale**

The **clinical scales** measure various aspects of personality and include:

**Hypochondriasis scale**

**Depression scale**

**Hysteria scale**

**Psychopathic deviate scale**

**Masculinity/femininity scale**

**Paranoia scale**

**Psychasthenia scale**

**Schizophrenia scale**

**Hypomania scale**

**Social introversion scale**

Although most of the original items were kept, the MMPI-2 resulted in a deletion of some statements from the original version. For instance, all items pertaining to religion and most of the questions about sexual practices were deleted. Other statements were reworded to update obsolete language, to make them more understandable, and to correct sexist language. Although the basic clinical scales were not changed, **content scales** that relate to substance abuse, eating disorders, Type-A behavior, repression, anger, cynicism, low self-esteem, family problems, and inability to function in a job were added.

The MMPI-2 can be scored by computer. A high score on any one of the scales does not necessarily mean that a person has a problem or psychological disorder. People with most types of disorders show elevated scores on several MMPI-2 scales. Psychologists look at patterns of scores to determine problem areas. Thus, the interpretation of MMPI scores is quite complicated.

Research has shown that the MMPI-2 is a reliable test that is easy to administer and score and is inexpensive to use.

Although the MMPI-2 is the most popular and widely used personality test for diagnosing psychological problems (it has been translated into 115 languages), it is not without its critics. For instance, the MMPI-2 does not reveal differences among normal personalities very well. As mentioned previously, interpretation of results is a complex process.

## Problem Solving Examples:

 What is the Minnesota Multiphasic Personality Inventory (MMPI-2) and what is it designed to measure?

The Minnesota Multiphasic Personality Inventory-2 (MMPI-2) is a self-report personality test. It was originally designed to discriminate between "normals" and people in psychiatric categories. It is now also used to assess an individual's personality.

The MMPI consists of 567 statements to which the subject is asked to answer true, false, or cannot say in respect to himself. If the subject responds that he "cannot say" too many times, his test record is considered invalid. Examples of typical statements on the MMPI include:

"I do not tire quickly."

"I am worried about sexual matters."

"I believe I am being plotted against."

"I am sure I am being talked about."

"I get mad easily and then get over it soon."

"I wish I could be as happy as others seem to be."

The statements on the MMPI-2 are divided into ten scales based on psychiatric categories. These scales are as follows: hypochondriasis, depression, hysteria, psychopathic deviate, masculinity-femininity, paranoia, psychasthenia (troubled with excessive fears and compulsive tendencies to dwell on certain ideas), schizophrenia, hypomania (tending to be physically and mentally overactive), and social introversion. In addition to these scales there are three validity scales which represent checks on lying, carelessness, defensiveness, etc. The lie scale consists of statements in which a particular answer (either true or false) is socially desirable but also extremely unlikely. For instance, "I never lie." The test is considered invalid for individuals who score too highly on any of these validity scales.

Each statement on the MMPI, except for those on the validity scales, is rated plus (+) or minus (–) on one or several scales. A plus means that answering "true" indicates that the subject agrees with the answer to that question given by most individuals who have been diagnosed as having a particular disorder. Many of the items are not "crazy" items. Their meaning is derived empirically without concern for the manifest meaning of the item. For example, the item "I would like to ride a horse" discriminates between several classifications, yet clinicians have no completely satisfactory explanation for why this would be so. The number of pluses and minuses on each scale is tallied and a profile is constructed for the individual. The profile should be interpreted with great care. The MMPI-2 has a high degree of empirical validity. The items (statements) were originally selected on the basis of whether or not they differentiated between normals and people who were specifically diagnosed as depressives, schizophrenics, paranoics, etc. Statements were eliminated if they were unuseful in differentiation. Thus, the MMPI-2 is considered to have a high degree of criterion-related validity (which is quite important for a personality inventory). The

MMPI-2 represents a re-standardization from the original norms, which were based on a small sample taken in Minnesota in the 1950s. The standardization sample may be quite uncharacteristic of the general population today.

 What are the advantages and disadvantages of projective testing?

Many psychologists argue that responses on a projective test may provide more valid and reliable personality data on a particular individual. Answers to questionnaires can be "faked" for the purposes of avoiding damage to the self-esteem. Moreover, since theoretically many impulses are censored by the ego, they are not available to consciousness; these aspects of the personality will not be able to be determined on a questionnaire because there is no means of "symbolic expression." Repressed impulses can find a means of expression only symbolically (e.g., dreams, parapraxes). Projective testing allows symbolic expression of conflicts and impulses. Tests like the Thematic Apperception Test (TAT) allow the subject to create an entire story, in theory symbolically representing his conflicts. Often subjects are told that a particular projective test is one of imagination or artistic ability so that the subject becomes "task-centered" rather than "self-centered." The subject is less inhibited and the responses are not distorted by "ego censorship."

Unlike an objective questionnaire, the projective test is unstructured. The subject truly has to search and think of an original answer; he cannot usually respond with conventional and stereotyped answers. Moreover, on a projective test the subject has the advantage of being able to modify and expand on his answers.

Some psychologists claim that projective tests also have the advantage of being pan-cultural because they demand no literacy or academic skills. Unfortunately, this may not be true. Associations typically used to interpret data are applicable only to people who are part of the culture in which these associations were originally derived. An answer that is frequent and "normal" in one culture may be infrequent and bizarre in another.

Other psychologists argue that projective tests provide a view of the total functioning individual whereas many objective tests measure only one trait. Projective tests claim to maintain the integrity and organization of the total personality (the Gestalt). However, there are objective tests, the MMPI, for example, which provide data on many different traits and yield diagnoses in a form similar to the projective tests.

One of the most serious disadvantages of projective tests is the possibility of examiner bias. Often examiners have pre-established views of subjects because of case-history reports. As a result they may produce interpretations which corroborate their pre-established opinions.

The interpretations of projective tests are open to much deserved criticism. The associations that an examiner makes between a given response and a given diagnosis may not be empirically supported. There is no scientific or statistical proof that these associations correlate with instances of particular diagnoses. Although psychologists have amassed a great deal of data on the frequencies of various responses, infrequent responses are by no means necessarily "crazy" responses, nor do particular responses reliably discriminate between normal and disturbed individuals. Thus, the standardized interpretations are often no more than common sense, unscientific speculations. Many of the projective tests cannot be said to be standardized in any rigorous way. Projective tests are in essence no better and no worse than the clinician who evaluates the responses. They may be quite useful to the experienced and insightful clinician, but of little use to the inexperienced tester.

One of the presumed advantages of the projective tests is that the subject is not aware of the purpose of the test and thus he lets down his defenses and his responses are undistorted. He does not "fake" his responses. Currently, the Rorschach and TAT tests are so well known that it is unlikely that a subject would not know that his personality was being assessed. It is likely that he would be even more defensive than on a questionnaire like the MMPI.

### 3.3.2 Projective Testing

**Projective tests** are personality tests that present an ambiguous stimulus that subjects are asked to describe or explain. The assumption is that people respond by projecting their own inner thoughts, feelings, fears, or conflicts into the test materials.

The two most famous projective tests are the Rorschach Inkblot Test and the Thematic Apperception Test.

Swiss psychiatrist **Hermann Rorschach** developed the **Rorschach Inkblot Test** in 1921.

This test consists of ten inkblots – half in black and white and half in color – that subjects are asked to describe. The examiner then goes through the cards again and asks questions to clarify what the subject has reported.

Five different scoring systems exist for scoring Rorschach responses. Responses can be analyzed in terms of content, whether the subject uses the whole inkblot or just part of it, originality, and the feature of the inkblot that determined the response. The examiner also considers whether the subject saw movement, human figures, animal figures, etc. in the inkblots.

The Rorschach continues to be widely used in clinical circles. Its advocates feel that the freedom of response encouraged by this test makes it an important clinical tool.

Critics, however, point out that the Rorschach has yet to demonstrate adequate reliability and validity and relies too heavily on interpretations made by the examiner.

The figure on the next page is an example of an inkblot used in the Rorschach test.

The **Thematic Apperception Test (TAT)** is a projective test that was developed by **Henry Murray** and his colleagues in 1935.

**Rorschach Inkblot**

The TAT consists of one blank card and nineteen other cards showing vague or ambiguous black-and-white drawings of human figures in various situations. The examiner chooses ten or fewer cards and presents them one at a time. Subjects are asked to tell a story about each card. As with the Rorschach, it is assumed that a person projects her/his own unconscious thoughts and feelings into her/his story.

The test's results are analyzed according to Murray's list of needs, which includes the need for achievement, affiliation, and aggression. Responses to each story are scored in terms of heroes, needs, themes, and outcome to provide insight into the subject's personality.

The TAT is time-consuming and difficult to administer. It relies heavily on the interpretation skills of the examiner and has not demonstrated adequate reliability and validity. It may also reflect a person's temporary motivational state and neglect more permanent aspects of personality.

### 3.3.3 Behavioral Assessment

Behavioral assessment attempts to obtain more objective information about personality by observing an individual's behavior directly. The assumption is that personality cannot be evaluated apart from the environment.

Behavioral assessment is a technique favored by behaviorists.

One method of behavioral assessment is **naturalistic observation,** which is the systematic recording of behavior in the natural environment, usually by trained observers.

Behavioral assessment can also occur outside of a natural setting. For instance, behavior may be assessed in a clinical setting or when a therapist has modified some aspect of the environment and observes its effect on behavior.

## Quiz: Personality – Assessing Intelligence and Personality

1.  According to Freud, the id develops

    (A)  at birth.

    (B)  around 6 months of age.

    (C)  around 1 to 2 years of age.

    (D)  around 6 years of age.

2.  A mother feeling resentment toward a child is overly cautious and protective of the child. This is an example of what type of defense mechanism?

    (A)  Repression

    (B)  Rationalization

    (C)  Reaction formation

    (D)  Sublimation

3.  Criticisms of the behavioral perspective of personality include all of the following EXCEPT:

    (A)  They do not consider possible unconscious motives or internal dispositions or traits that might be consistent from situation to situation.

    (B)  Historically, they have relied too much on animal research.

    (C)  They have not paid attention to possible enduring qualities of personality.

(D) They have focused more on cognition and less on personality.

4. Maslow's hierarchy of needs occurs in what order:

(A) physiological, safety, love and belongingness, esteem, and self-actualization

(B) self-actualization, physiological, safety, esteem, and love and belongingness

(C) safety, love and belongingness, physiological, esteem, and self-actualization

(D) physiological, love and belongingness, safety, self-actualization, esteem

5. According to Sheldon, people who are endomorphs tend to have what type of personality?

(A) They tend to be energetic, assertive, and courageous.

(B) They tend to be sociable, relaxed, and love to eat.

(C) They tend to be restrained, fearful, and artistic.

(D) They tend to be humorless and mean spirited.

6. Who proposed a triarchic theory of intelligence that specifies three important parts of intelligence: componential, experiential, and contextual intelligence?

(A) Charles Spearman

(B) Raymond Cattell

(C) Robert Sternberg

(D) Howard Gardner

7. To calculate IQ,

   (A) a child's chronological age is divided by his/her mental age and multiplied by 100.

   (B) a child's mental age is divided by his/her chronological age and multiplied by 100.

   (C) a child's mental age and chronological age are added together and then divided by 100.

   (D) a child's mental age and chronological age are added together and then multiplied by 100.

8. The most widely used self-report inventory is

   (A) MMPI-2.

   (B) Rorschach Inkblot Test.

   (C) Thematic Apperception Test.

   (D) None of the above.

9. A person who is classified as being mildly retarded falls into an IQ range of

   (A) less than 20.

   (B) 20-34.

   (C) 35-49.

   (D) 50-70.

10. Giftedness is often defined as having an IQ between

    (A)  100 and 110.

    (B)  110 and 120.

    (C)  120 and 130.

    (D)  None of the above.

## ANSWER KEY

| | | | |
|---|---|---|---|
| 1. | (A) | 6. | (C) |
| 2. | (C) | 7. | (B) |
| 3. | (D) | 8. | (A) |
| 4. | (A) | 9. | (D) |
| 5. | (B) | 10. | (C) |

# CHAPTER 4

# Motivation and Emotion

## 4.1 Motivation

Psychologists study motivation because they want to know why a behavior occurs. Motivation is the process that initiates, directs, and sustains behavior while simultaneously satisfying physiological or psychological needs. A **motive** is a reason or purpose for behavior.

## Problem Solving Example:

**Q** What is motivation?

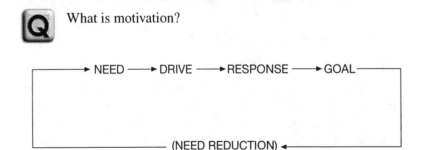

**A** The field of psychology concerned particularly with the factors that influence the arousal, direction and persistence of behavior is called the psychology of motivation. Why does one child perform well in school while another does not? Why does one person choose to be a doctor and another a mason? Why is one person attracted to a life of crime and another to one of altruism? In other words, why do people behave as they do? These questions demonstrate that motivation is important in human life. It is only recently that the study of motivation has been subject to empirical investigations.

The concept of motivation in psychological theory has been fragmented for decades. It is generally agreed that motives are energizers of behavior, but how they operate or originate is a continuing source of debate. Each theorist supposes different motivational states. There are the basic biological drives such as hunger, thirst, and sex. There are the learned motives such as affiliation, achievement, competitiveness. There are emotional motives such as pleasure – from a mild pleasing sensation to ecstasy – and pain, including anger, fear and frustration. All of these are potential motivators for behavior.

The research in this area has generally focused on one particular state. Though motives are studied individually they are often examined in regard to their interaction with other processes such as learning, conditioning, perception or social interaction. In addition to the study of particular motives, there has been increasing interest in the effect a motivational state has on other psychological processes such as learning and remembering. This direction of research has begun to expand and at the same time connect the varying theoretical schools.

### 4.1.1 Theories of Motivation

Several theories describe the basis for motivation.

An **instinct** is an inborn, unlearned, fixed pattern of behavior that is biologically determined and is characteristic of an entire species. The idea of attributing human and animal behavior to instincts was not seriously considered until **Charles Darwin** suggested that humans evolved from lower animals.

**William McDougall** believed that instincts were "the prime movers of all human activity." He identified 18 instincts, including parental instinct, curiosity, escape, reproduction, self-assertion, pugnacity, and gregariousness. However, psychologists do not agree on what and how many human instincts there are. While McDougall suggested 18, others suggested even more.

Instinct theory was widely accepted by psychologists for the first 20 or 30 years of the 20th century. Today, the idea that motivation is based on instincts has been replaced by other theories because psychologists recognized that human behavior is too diverse and unpredictable to be consistent across our species. Further, there is no scientific way to prove the existence of instincts in humans. Many feel that instinct theory provides a description rather than an explanation of behavior.

## Problem Solving Example:

 What is an instinct?

It was with the work of Darwin that the concept of "instinct" became important to the study of human behavior. During Darwin's time, the term "instinct" referred to behaviors that were not acquired through learning and experience but that were provided for in the organism's biological structure. It was proposed that on their first appearance, these behaviors are performed, if not perfectly, at least well enough to secure the survival of the individual. This formulation gave rise to a great deal of controversy during the first half of this century between those who adhered to the earlier philosophic idea that instinct was a natural urge to maintain life and seek happiness and those who entertained the possibility that complex behaviors have an innate origin.

The work of William McDougall was especially important in classifying and understanding instincts. McDougall proposed that each instinct is receptive to certain stimuli and contains a disposition to behave in a certain way. He further argued that the receptivity and behavioral components of each instinct might change as a function of learning. He maintained that each instinct has an emotional core that will not change with experience. Therefore, as one becomes older, an instinct might be activated by different stimuli and produce many different behaviors, but the emotional component will remain the same. He generated a list that paired each instinct with an emotion. For example, flight was paired with fear and pugnacity was paired with anger.

During the early part of the last century, hundreds of "instinct" theorists published long lists of new "instincts" and proposed that these were the determinants of the arousal and direction of behavior. There was no attempt to measure the predictability of these instincts and the sole criterion for inclusion in the lists was the opinion of the particular psychologist who was formulating each list. It is no wonder that this procedure fell into disrepute. Consequently, theories about instincts underwent extensive revisions. Today, it is generally accepted that innate tendencies interact with experience to produce behavior.

**Drive-reduction theory** was popularized by **Clark Hull** and suggests that motivation results from attempting to keep a balanced internal state.

**Homeostasis** is the built-in tendency to maintain internal stability or equilibrium. Any deviation from homeostasis creates a **need**. A need results in a drive for action. A **drive**, therefore, is a psychological state of tension or arousal that motivates activities to reduce this tension and restore homeostatic balance.

**Primary drives** are drives that arise from biological needs. **Secondary drives** are learned through operant or classical conditioning.

## Problem Solving Example:

Make the distinction between primary and secondary sources of drive giving examples of each.

When speaking about motivational variables a distinction is often made between primary and secondary drive sources. Generally, primary sources of drive are associated with innate bodily mechanisms. These drive sources are sometimes called homeostatic, biogenic, or physiogenic. Examples of stimuli having a primary motivational effect are food, water, air, temperature and almost any intense stimuli such as loud noises and electric shocks.

All secondary sources of drive are learned. These are acquired drives – responses that have been acquired in a particular environmental situation. These responses have motivational consequences similar to the primary sources. That is, they influence and direct behavior. Today, much of human behavior is thought to depend upon acquired drives. For this reason, they have been of special importance to the psychologist. These sources of drive include such learned desires as success, power, affection, money, appearance, and security. Some theorists believe that fear, anxiety and certain verbal cues are also learned drives.

In modern culture it is no longer common to experience hunger, thirst, or great amounts of pain. What is it then that motivates the great amounts of activity in any large metropolitan area? Acquired drives appear to be central to any explanation of modern life.

Drive-reduction theory can be diagrammed as:

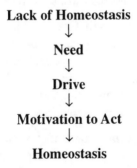

**Lack of Homeostasis**
↓
**Need**
↓
**Drive**
↓
**Motivation to Act**
↓
**Homeostasis**

For instance, homeostasis works to maintain a constant internal body temperature in humans of approximately 98.6 degrees Fahrenheit. If body temperature goes above this average temperature, our bodies automatically respond (e.g., perspiration) to restore equilibrium. These automatic responses may not be sufficient by themselves, and we may be motivated to take other actions (e.g., remove some clothing).

The nervous systems are involved in maintaining homeostasis. For instance, the **parasympathetic branch** acts to counteract heat and the **sympathetic branch** responds to cold. Both of these branches are governed by the **hypothalamus,** a structure found near the base of the forebrain that is involved in the regulation of basic biological needs (e.g., temperature, hunger, thirst).

Drive theories, however, cannot explain all motivation. Motivation can exist without drive arousal. For instance, we often eat when there is no need to eat (i.e., we are not physically hungry).

**Incentive theories** propose that external stimuli regulate motivational states (e.g., the sight of a hot fudge sundae motivates eating), and that human behavior is goal-directed. That is, anticipated rewards (i.e., the taste of the sundae) can direct and encourage behavior. Rewards, in motivational terms, are incentives, and behavior is goal-directed to obtain these rewards. Incentives vary from person to person and can change over time.

Many psychologists believe that instead of contradicting each other, drive and incentive theories may work together in motivating behavior.

**Arousal theory** suggests that the aim of motivation is to maintain an optimal level of arousal. **Arousal** is a person's state of alertness and mental and physical activation. If arousal is less than the optimal level, we do something to stimulate it. If arousal is greater than the optimal level, we seek to reduce the stimulation. The level of arousal considered optimal varies from person to person.

The **Yerkes-Dodson law** states that a particular level of motivational arousal produces optimal performance on a task. Research suggests that people perform best when arousal is moderate. On easy or simple tasks, people can perform better under higher levels of arousal. On difficult or complex tasks, the negative effects of over–arousal are particularly strong.

**Richard Solomon** proposed an **opponent-process theory** of motivation. This theory argues that one emotional state will trigger an opposite emotional state that lasts long after the original emotion has disappeared. That is, an increase in arousal will produce a calming reaction in the nervous system, and vice versa. It is the opponent process, not the initial reaction, therefore, that maintains the motivation to carry out certain behaviors.

For instance, opponent-process theory suggests that the fear that skydivers feel when risking their lives will trigger an extremely positive emotional response. As a consequence, the motivation to skydive increases. This theory has also been used to explain the motivation behind risky, dangerous behaviors such as drug addiction.

## Problem Solving Examples:

 Discuss the relationship between arousal and motivation.

Many psychologists regard arousal level as the central aspect of motivation. Various motives have different goals: food, water, shelter, etc. The common element is the arousal of the motivated organism. The more highly motivated the organism, the greater the level of arousal. In theories of human motivation, arousal level is used as a measure, as an indicator, of the strength of a motive. Because of this, arousal level is often considered a central aspect of all types of motivation: emotional, physiological, etc.

In the association or neobehavioristic theory of learning, the probability of a response is the product of two general factors, one of which is called drive (D), the general level of arousal.

 Discuss the relationship between arousal level and performance.

In general, increased arousal level or drive level produces improved performance in animals and humans on simple tasks. Several studies have indicated this to be the case. Bills (1927), for example, found that when tension level is increased in a subject by having him squeeze hard objects, performance was improved for such tasks as memorization, addition, and naming letters. Several animal studies have shown that increased arousal, produced by food or water deprivation, greatly improves performance in learning tasks.

An extremely high level of arousal, however, can impair performance in situations that require discrimination among cues or responding appropriately at different times. (In simpler terms: very complex tasks.) Expressed graphically, the relationship between level of arousal and level of cue discrimination is an inverted U-shape. Up to a certain point, as arousal level increases, so does cue discrimination ability or performance level. This rise in the graph represents an increased ability to discriminate among cues of increasing complexity, as alertness, interest, and positive emotion are increased. After the optimum level – the apex of the inverted U – is reached, as arousal level becomes greater, there is an increase in anxiety and emotional disturbances, and, at the same time, performance declines. This phenomenon is called the Yerkes-Dodson effect after its discoverers.

College students in testing situations who tend to have very high levels of anxiety often do not perform as well as students who have lower anxiety levels. The reason, of course, is that insofar as exams are a "complex task" students who are overly anxious are more anxious than the optimal level of anxiety allows.

**Abraham Maslow**, a humanistic theorist, proposed a **hierarchy of needs** to explain motivations. The figure on the next page presents this hierarchy in its pyramidal form.

According to Maslow, human needs are arranged in a hierarchy. People must satisfy their **basic** or **physiological needs** before they can satisfy their **higher-order needs**. Individuals progress upward in the hierarchy when lower needs are satisfied, but they may regress to lower levels if basic needs are no longer satisfied. As one moves up the hierarchy, each level of needs becomes less biological and more social in origin.

For instance, Maslow proposed that the basic, fundamental needs essential for survival, such as food, water, stable body temperature, etc. must be met first. When a person satisfies a level of physiological needs, this satisfaction activates needs at the next level. This means that after basic **physiological needs** are met, **safety and security needs** become motivating.

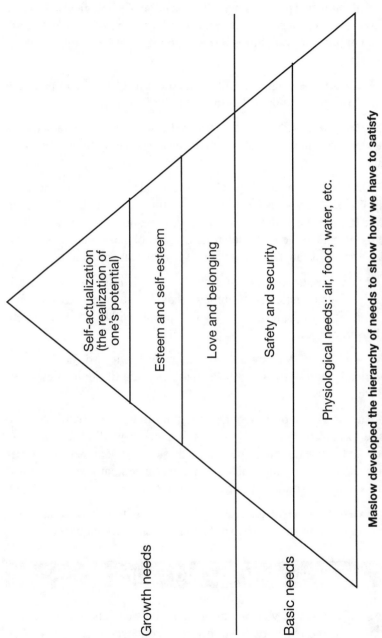

**Maslow developed the hierarchy of needs to show how we have to satisfy certain basic needs before we can satisfy higher growth needs.**

Self-actualization (the realization of one's potential)

Esteem and self-esteem

Love and belonging

Safety and security

Physiological needs: air, food, water, etc.

Growth needs

Basic needs

Following this pattern, only when the basic physiological and safety needs are met can a person consider fulfilling higher-order needs, consisting of **love and belonging, esteem and self-esteem**, and **self-actualization**.

**Love and belonging** needs include the need to obtain and give affection and to be a contributing member of society.

**Esteem and self-esteem** relate to the need to develop a sense of self-worth by knowing that others are aware of one's competence and value.

The highest need in Maslow's motivational hierarchy is the need for **self-actualization**, which is the need to fulfill one's potential. According to Maslow, people will be frustrated if they are unable to fully use their talents or pursue their true interests. A state of self-actualization provides a sense of satisfaction with one's current state of affairs.

Psychologists feel that Maslow's theory is important because it highlights the complexity of human needs. It also emphasizes that basic biological needs must be met before people will be concerned with higher-order needs.

Criticisms of Maslow's theory include that it is difficult to test empirically; terms such as self-actualization are difficult to measure and study.

**Burton White** proposed the notion of **intrinsic motivation** or the desire to perform an activity for itself because we find it inherently enjoyable. For example, a person reads several books per month because she/he finds it enjoyable. Activities carried out because of curiosity are also examples of intrinsic motivation.

**Extrinsic motivation** occurs when an activity is performed in order to obtain a reward or to avoid an undesirable consequence.

## Problem Solving Example:

**Q** How would Maslow differentiate between an individual who was motivated by lower needs and one who was motivated by self-actualization needs?

**A** Maslow's Hierarchy of Needs theory proposes five motivational levels that direct human behavior in a hierarchical manner. The most basic needs are physiological, these are followed by safety and security needs, love and belonging, self-esteem and finally, self-actualization needs. As one need is satisfied, the next in the hierarchy becomes the important motivating factor. According to Maslow, there is a marked difference between the behavior patterns of people motivated by lower needs (deficiency-oriented) and those motivated by self-actualization needs (growth-oriented). The deficiency-oriented person can be contrasted to the growth-oriented individual on a number of different behavior characteristics.

The person who is still motivated to satisfy lower needs is characterized by a tendency to be self-centered and concerned with his own needs, to reject his own impulses, to seek goals that are common to many others, to look for gratifications that are relatively short-term and temporary, to seek gratification that results in tension-reduction, to behave mainly on the basis of external cues, and to view others in terms of how they can satisfy his needs.

On the other hand, the growth-oriented person is likely to be more concerned with the nature of the world at large and other people than with himself, to be accepting of his impulses, to attain goals that are individualistic and unique to him, to be attracted to gratifications that lead to permanent and long-term change, to behave from internal rather than external cues, and to view people for what they are, not as potential subjects he can utilize to satisfy his needs.

This picture of the self-actualizing individual may be partly responsible for the increasing number of mental health therapists who have adopted Maslow's theory or some variant of it as a goal model for their patients. Self-actualizing behavior is clearly that of an optimally developed individual. Before Maslow's conceptualization of the term through his study of exceptional individuals, the literature was scarce in its descriptions of healthy behavior and heavy in its concentration of pathological tendencies. It was Maslow who formally introduced to psychology the model of a healthy, optimally functioning individual.

That so many have adopted his theoretical stance is evidence of the need that existed for the work he has done.

## 4.1.2  Human Needs

Motives for several of the most important human needs – hunger, thirst, sexuality – have been studied by psychologists.

What motivates us to eat? What motivates us to stop eating once we have begun? How do we know we are hungry? Psychologists have attempted to answer these and other questions related to hunger and motivation.

Researchers have found that people report that they are hungry even when their stomachs have been removed for medical reasons. The explanation for hunger, therefore, is more complex than an empty stomach. A feeling of hunger seems to be related to both the brain and body chemistry as well as to external factors.

**Glucose** is a simple sugar nutrient that provides energy. When the level of glucose in our bloodstream is low, we feel hungry. When glucose levels are high, we feel full. Blood glucose levels appear to be monitored by **glucostats**, neurons that are sensitive to glucose levels. Where these glucostats are located is not clear, although it seems likely that the **hypothalamus** receives messages about glucose levels.

Another body chemical, **insulin**, is also related to hunger. Insulin is important for converting blood glucose into stored fat. Insulin is a hormone secreted by the pancreas. Research has shown that insulin influences hunger indirectly by decreasing glucose levels. Research has also shown that people with elevated insulin levels report feeling hungry and usually eat more than those with normal insulin levels.

One theory holds that the **hypothalamus** is the brain structure that appears to be primarily responsible for food intake. Injury to the hypothalamus, for instance, can cause radical changes in eating patterns. Laboratory rats whose **lateral hypothalamus** (**LH,** located at the side of the hypothalamus) was damaged, would often literally starve themselves to death. When the rats' LH was stimulated, however, they would overeat.

Rats with injury to the **ventromedial hypothalamus** (**VMH**, located toward the center of the hypothalamus) became extreme overeaters. VMH stimulation caused animals to stop eating.

The **dual-center theory** maintains that the hypothalamus contains an "on" and an "off" switch for eating located in two different regions, the LH and VMH. These switches can be activated by internal (e.g., damage or stimulation) and external signals (e.g., sight or taste of food).

Some researchers have suggested that injury to the hypothalamus affects the weight **set point** that regulates food intake. The weight set point is the particular or target weight that the body strives to maintain. Hunger or food intake adjusts to meet this set point. This means whenever we are below our set point, we feel hungry until we gain weight to match our set point.

Set point theory has been used as one explanation for obesity. According to set point theory, each person's body has a fixed number of **fat cells**, the cells that store fat. Fat cells may shrink in size when a dieter loses weight and increase in size when weight is gained. The number of fat cells does not change, only their size changes. Some researchers propose that the shriveled fat cells that result from dieting send hunger messages to the dieter's brain.

To make matters worse, a dieter's **metabolism** (the rate at which energy is produced and expended by the body) may slow down as a result of a decrease in fat cell size. It is harder to lose weight with a slow metabolism.

Some individuals seem to naturally have a slow metabolism and even though they eat small amounts of food, they gain weight readily. Those who gain weight easily are actually biologically more efficient because they easily convert food into body tissue.

Other individuals seem to naturally have a high metabolism rate and can eat as much as they want without weight gain. These individuals are inefficient in using the food that they eat and much of it is wasted.

There is also evidence that some people have a **genetic predisposition** to become obese. It seems likely that metabolic rate is an important inherited factor.

Other reasons for eating and overeating include:

| | |
|---|---|
| **Learned preferences and habits** | We learn not only when to eat and how much to eat at one time but many taste preferences are the result of experience. |
| **External cues** | External cues can influence eating. External cues can include the sight or smell of food as well as time of day. |
| **Stress and arousal** | Several research studies have shown a relationship between heightened arousal and overeating for some people. |

**Anorexia nervosa** is an eating disorder that is characterized by an irrational pursuit of thinness and an overconcern with body image and gaining weight. Anorexics feel fat even when they look emaciated. They often are literally starving themselves to death. About 95% of people with anorexia nervosa are females.

**Bulimia** or **binge** eating occurs when people consume huge amounts of food in a short period of time, usually secretly. Following the binge, bulimics often engage in self-induced vomiting, vigorous exercise, laxative-abuse or other methods to **purge** themselves of the food consumed. Most bulimics maintain a normal weight.

Because we lose a significant amount of water through sweating and urination, thirst represents an important motivational drive.

Three primary internal mechanisms produce thirst. First, when the concentration of **salt cells** in the body reaches a certain level, the hypothalamus is triggered to act in a way that results in the experience of thirst.

A decrease in the total volume of fluid in the **circulatory system** also causes the sense of thirst.

Finally, a rise in body temperature or a significant energy expenditure also produces thirst, probably because of a rise in the salt concentration of the body.

The dry mouth that accompanies thirst is a symptom of the need for water but not the cause. The body does seem to have a kind of water meter in the mouth and stomach, however, that monitors the amount of water that has been consumed and immediately informs drinkers when they have had enough liquid to meet their needs.

## Problem Solving Examples:

 What experimental evidence is there that brain mechanisms of motivation are responsible for controlling hunger and thirst?

If a well-fed animal is placed in a chamber with food that it normally prefers, it will not eat it. If, however, the experimenter turns on an apparatus designed to stimulate an electrode planted in the animal's mid-brain, the animal will proceed to eat. In fact, if the electrode has been properly placed, the animal will eat for as long as the stimulation continues. Furthermore, the animal does not just eat anything. His response is identical to that which accompanies the normal biological hunger drive. He is motivated and behaves in the same way as he does when he is hungry. Similar responses have been discovered in a variety of animals for different motivational systems including thirst and reproductive behavior.

While stimulating particular regions of the brain causes an animal to eat, destroying the same region can produce an animal who has no desire for food, even when deprived for long periods of time. Likewise, if stimulating a particular area of the brain causes the animal to stop eating, a lesion in that spot will produce an animal that will not stop eating and appears to be chronically hungry. While psychologists can now control a number of motivational responses through electrical stimulation and surgical procedures, the mechanisms that underlie these responses are still unknown.

**Q** How is the esophagus bypass used to study the motivational processes involved in hunger and thirst?

**A** The digestive system of most organisms is slow, requiring two hours or more to convert a meal into biochemical units for metabolic use. Therefore, many animals, including man, rely on sensing devices that signal when enough food or water has been consumed. These signals come long before a change in the biochemical state can trigger the brain mechanisms to stop eating or drinking.

Some psychologists guessed that a reasonable place for the location of receptors for monitoring the intake of food and drink are somewhere in the mouth or throat area. These researchers designed an experimental device that would help them indicate whether an animal would eat normally even if the food did not reach his stomach. This device is known as the esophageal bypass. Theoretically, the animal should eat and drink normally and then stop even though no food or drink has gone further than the mouth and throat. Later, when the consumption motivation system discovers that its estimation had been incorrect, it should again produce eating and drinking behavior in the animal. This is precisely what happens with experimental animals. Placed on a food and drink deprivation schedule and allowed to eat and drink only every 24 hours, the regular habits of the animal are carefully noted. Then the esophagus bypass operation is performed, and once again the animal is placed on the 24-hour deprivation schedule.

A thirsty animal will perform precisely as the theory predicts. He will drink his normal fill and stop. Five or ten minutes later he will drink again, this time more than the first, and then stop. This cycle continues with the amount of water consumed increasing as the deficit increases with time.

A hungry animal, however, will continue eating – sometimes up to 80% of its body weight (dogs). From these findings, it is clear that if a mechanism exists for shutting off hunger it is not in the mouth and throat area. Further experiments have determined that the feedback mechanism for shutting off hunger is somewhere in the upper ingestional tract or the stomach itself.

Unlike food and water, sex is not necessary for individual survival, but is necessary for the survival of the species. Sexual motivation can arise out of social, cultural, and biological motives.

Although not essential for survival, sexual motivation is very strong in humans. Even though social and cultural factors play a more important role in human sexual behavior, **hormones** have important organizational and activational effects. In humans, the hypothalamus controls the release of **luteinizing hormone (LH)** from the **pituitary gland**. LH controls the release of masculinizing (**androgens**) and feminizing (**estrogens and progestins**) hormones from the ovaries and testes. The hypothalamus, therefore, apparently plays a role in regulating the sex drive by sensing hormone levels and affecting their secretion through pituitary gland stimulation.

**Hormonal factors** affect sexual behavior less in more physiologically advanced species. Hormones do control sexual behavior in lower mammals – they mate only during **ovulation** (the monthly release of an egg from the ovary) when the female secretes **pheromones**, which attract the male.

**Heterosexuals** are attracted to individuals of the opposite sex.

**Homosexuals** are attracted to individuals of the same sex.

**Bisexuals** are attracted to people of the same and opposite sexes.

No one theory fully explains why people develop a particular sexual orientation. Some theories are **biological** in nature, suggesting that there may be a genetic or hormonal reason. Others have suggested that **environmental** factors play a key role. Still others argue that sex-role orientation is a **learned behavior**. Some feel that **childhood experiences** and **family factors** are important.

## Problem Solving Example:

Is sexual behavior an innate or learned motivating factor? Discuss.

**A** Though sexual behavior has often been classified as instinctual, there has been growing interest in the view that it is at least partially a learned drive. If it was completely innate it would not be readily manipulable by altering the internal or external state of the organism, which recent experimentation has proven possible.

Though the mating season for animals is thought to be innate, it has been shown that by altering the amount of artificial light to which they are exposed (cats for instance), can be made to demonstrate mating behavior in November and December though their usual season is from February to June. Experiments have also been done with certain varieties of fish to demonstrate that the presence of certain external cues is necessary for sexual behavior to take place. One type of fish, the stickleback male, displays sexual behavior only at the sight of a female fish with a swollen abdomen. These females contain eggs and when they are seen by the male fish, he begins nest-building behavior. A model of such a female fish also evokes this behavior in the male, while a slim model does not.

The role of experience in sexual activity also lends support to the idea that sexuality is at least partially learned. While sexually mature rats that have been reared in isolation show normal copulation activity, monkeys and apes with the same background fare poorly. It appears that the position of an animal on the phylogenetic scale is important in determining how much learning influences its sexuality. Though it was for a long time thought of as a primary (or innate) biological drive, sexual behavior is more easily influenced by the learning process than are hunger and thirst, which are essential for the survival of the individual organism. In the higher animals, at least, the survival of the species is somewhat more dependent on the particular experiences of the individual members of the group under study.

### 4.1.3  Achievement Motivation

**Social motives** are conditions that direct people toward establishing or maintaining relationships with others. Social motives are learned through socialization and cultural conditioning.

Social needs are internal conditions related to feelings about self or others and establishing and maintaining relationships.

The **need for achievement (nAch)** is a social need that directs a person to constantly strive for excellence and success.

**Henry Murray** identified a number of social motives or needs and believed that people have these social motives in differing degrees. He developed the **Thematic Apperception Test (TAT)** (described in chapter 3) to measure the strength of these various needs. The **need for achievement** was included on Murray's list of needs and was defined as the need to accomplish something difficult and to perform at a high standard of excellence.

**David McClelland** and others have been interested in the effects of high or low needs for achievement. They found that people with a **high nAch** tend to set goals of moderate difficulty. They pursue goals that are challenging yet attainable. They actively pursue present and future successes and are willing to take risks. They persist after repeated failures, plan for the future, and take pride in their success.

Achievement motivation appears to be learned and related to child-rearing practices and values in the home. Parents may be more likely to have children with high nAch if they give their children responsibilities, stress independence, and praise them for genuine accomplishments.

There is evidence that, at times, both men and women experience **fear of success**. **Fear of success** occurs when someone worries that success in competitive achievement situations will lead to unpleasant consequences (such as unpopularity).

## Problem Solving Examples:

**Q** Discuss McClelland's concept of Achievement Motive and the effect of nAch on individual behavior.

 **A** Why is it that some people are driven to succeed at what they do and others do not appear to have much interest in success or high-level performance? Why are some people unwilling to even undertake a task in which they have a good chance of succeeding? These questions are important, particularly in our success-oriented society. They have been of interest to psychologists for a long time because of their applicability to both work and school performance. The pioneer work in this area was carried out by David McClelland. He postulated that the achievement motive develops in some people and not in others because it is a producer of positive affect for some and of negative affect for others. An achievement environment produces positive affect when it produces outcomes that are only moderately discrepant from those previously experienced, and negative affect when its results are very different from previous experience. For example, a person who has scored high on achievement motivation would be predicted to approach, stay in, and perform well in situations with opportunities for achievement. This would occur mainly because achievement environments are not too different from the environments in which his previous learning has taken place. Individuals that measure low on need for achievement would find such situations negative and tend to avoid them and perform less effectively in them. Again, mainly because their past experience did not include much exposure to similar environments.

Since individuals differ in the amount of satisfaction they receive from achievement, it was further hypothesized that environments can be measured as providing more or less achievement opportunities. Achievement-oriented individuals prefer environments in which there is moderate risk, as achievement will not be experienced much in low risk situations nor is it likely to occur in high risk situations with very low probability of success. Feedback on performance is necessary to the achievement-oriented individual since it is important for him to know whether he has accomplished what he has set out to do. Finally, individual responsibility must be provided. The achievement-oriented person wishes to be seen as the one responsible for the result.

McClelland further hypothesized from his investigations that people with a high need for achievement are attracted to entrepreneurial pursuits for their lifetime occupation since such activities often afford an environment that contains all the ingredients necessary to produce high achievement stimulation. From this hypothesis, McClelland has developed theories concerning the economic growth and potential of countries based on the level of achievement-motivation of their inhabitants.

 Fear of failure is closely related to and often interferes with achievement motivation. Explain this statement.

The theory of achievement motivation, originally advanced by David McClelland, has been further developed by John Atkinson. Atkinson's most recent formulation describes two basic types of people, both of whom will respond in an achievement-oriented way, but the environments that will give rise to the greatest achievement behavior will be different for each group. The first group is comprised of individuals who are more motivated to achieve than they are to avoid failure; members of the second group are more motivated by the fear of failure than by the motive to achieve success. The first group experiences a pleasant affect from success, while the second group experiences a pleasant affect from avoiding failure.

An important point of consideration for an achievement-motivated individual is the degree of difficulty of the task involved. Some tasks have a high probability of success, such as $P = .9$, and other tasks have a low probability of success, such as $P = .1$. The greatest sense of achievement is supposedly derived from successful accomplishment of the more difficult tasks. Atkinson has postulated that individuals who are primarily motivated to achieve will perform best in situations with tasks of medium difficulty, $P = .5$. On the other hand, persons motivated by a fear of failure would be more likely to be attracted to tasks with an extremely high possibility of failure, $P = .05$ or with an extremely high chance of success, $P = .95$. In both cases the experience of failure would be mitigated. In the first because the task was so difficult that almost no one would be expected to succeed and in the second because chances of failure are minimal.

The situation that the high fear of failure individual avoids most is precisely that which the high nAch person would be most likely to approach – the medium-risk situation, $P = .5$. It is assumed that high fear of failure individuals would avoid all achievement-related tasks if it were possible, but when they find themselves in a situation where they must work on task-achievement, they will be attracted to extremely difficult or extremely easy tasks.

These theoretical predictions have produced intriguing, but confusing results. They have made it apparent that there is a need for refining and standardizing the measurement procedures.

## 4.2 Emotion

**Emotion** includes:

a subjective conscious experience or cognitive component;

bodily or physiological arousal; and

overt or behavioral expressions.

As humans, we use our emotions to **communicate** our feelings to others. Emotions are **automatic** and **involuntary**. They also guide our behavior and appear to be more complex in humans than in any other animal.

## Problem Solving Examples:

**Q** Define emotion in terms of feelings, responses, and motivation.

**A** Emotion can be broadly defined as a complex state of the organism, generally characterized by a heightened arousal level. The term emotion can be defined in three basic ways: in terms of feelings, responses, and motivation.

Davitz (1969) found that for most people, the term emotion applies to a particular set of feelings. A person feels anger if someone is offensive to him, pleasure if he receives a gift, or fear if a fierce animal is about to attack him. Behavioristic psychologists dislike defining emotion as feelings, since a feeling is a highly subjective state and cannot be measured objectively. As such, they are not likely to yield consistent data; and, in addition, they are difficult to organize. However, much recent work in organizing emotional feeling states has proved encouraging.

Emotion may also be thought of as a response. "Response" in this case refers not only to an overt behavior, but also to an internal process that occurs as a result of a particular stimulus, either external or internal, which is significant to the individual.

Emotion as a response has been viewed in two ways. First, some consider it a response to one's perception and judgment of a particular stimulus situation. For example, if a person perceives and judges a particular situation to be threatening, fear will be the emotional response. Other investigators supporting the (very early) position of William James see emotion as a response to physiological events that occur during a state of arousal. James suggested that emotions are responses to such bodily changes as increased heart rate and respiration.

Emotion can also be viewed in terms of motivation. To some investigators, emotion is identical to motivation. There are two ways to look at emotion in this light. First, emotions are seen as strong motives; an organism is induced or motivated to do something in order to eliminate the motive. In the case of rats, for example, Neal Miller showed that rats learn new responses in order to remove themselves from an environment in which they had been shocked. The anxiety that motivated them to learn the avoidance response was viewed by Miller both as an emotion and a motive.

Another view of emotion as motivation, proposed by Sylvan Tomkins, suggests that motives are important only when they are energized by emotional excitement or arousal. The motive specifies a goal associated with a particular physiological state, but this must be amplified by emotional excitement. In sexual motivation, for example, the motive is ineffective unless it is accompanied by emotional excitement.

 Discuss three indicators of emotion.

 There are three important indicators that are used to indicate emotion: personal reports, observed behaviors, and physiological indicators.

Personal reports include oral and written reports by subjects on their experiences. Outward response may not reveal an individual's feelings or arousal, but it can indicate the type of emotion experienced.

Emotion can be detected from observing behavior. Such behaviors include gestures, postures, facial expressions, movements, and other responses which help indicate the emotion being expressed.

Finally, emotion is indicated by physiological changes. Changes in heart rate, breathing pattern, blood pressure, pupil size, EEG pattern, or GSR (galvanic skin response) indicate arousal level and are often interpreted as an indication of an emotional state.

### 4.2.1  Elements of the Emotional Experience

Emotional reactions are associated with arousal of the **autonomic nervous system (ANS)**. The autonomic nervous system is a division of the **peripheral nervous system** that is concerned with involuntary functions of the body and regulates the activity of the glands, smooth muscles, and blood vessels. The autonomic nervous system is also responsible for the **flight-or-fight response** that occurs during emergency situations. When this response occurs, the pupils dilate, heart rate accelerates, respiration increases, adrenaline is secreted, and digestion is inhibited. The autonomic responses that accompany emotions, therefore, are controlled by the brain.

The **galvanic skin response (GSR)** describes an increase in electrical conductivity of the skin that occurs when the sweat glands increase their activity. GSR is often used as a measure of autonomic arousal and emotional reactions.

## Problem Solving Example:

 Do different emotional states produce different patterns of physiological change? Define directional fractionation.

 Research has not supported the idea that different emotional or arousal states yield differing bodily states. According to Lacey

(1967), most individuals show similar patterns of autonomic response to widely varying stressful situations.

Some investigators, however, have reported subtle differences in physical reactions among different emotional states. The most interesting and suggestive of these involves the phenomenon called directional fractionation. Directional fractionation can be defined as an autonomic reaction in which heart rate decreases (as in a parasympathetic reaction), while other changes occur in an opposite direction, such as increased skin conductance (GSR) as occurs in a sympathetic response). In a normal sympathetic arousal state, both heart rate and GSR would increase.

In studies where directional fractionation is induced, subjects usually take in external stimuli such as colors and patterns flashed before them or a tape recording of an actor portraying a man dying of injuries. In these situations, however, subjects do not actively react. A normal sympathetic arousal state would result if the individual had to actively react physically or even mentally, as in solving problems.

Despite such infrequent phenomena as directional fractionation, most variations in mood, arousal, or emotion are accompanied by similar bodily states.

The **polygraph** or **lie detector test** is based on the assumption that there is a link between lying and emotions. Lie detector tests measure respiration, heart rate, blood pressure, and the galvanic skin response. Lie detectors do not detect lies; instead they detect **nervousness** as measured by various physiological reactions. Usually lie detectors are accurate around two-thirds of the time, but many courts do not allow lie detector evidence. This is because some people may appear nervous when they are innocent and others may appear calm even though they are guilty.

## Problem Solving Example:

 Describe how a "lie detector" works. How is a lie detection test conducted?

**A** A lie detector (polygraph), used to ascertain an individual's guilt in a crime, is a device that detects and measures autonomic changes that accompany emotional experience. There are several variations of the lie detector, but practically all lie detectors measure blood pressure, respiration, and GSR. The assumption behind the use of the lie detector is that a person can hide external emotional expression, but not the involuntary, physiological changes that accompany it.

In a lie detection test, a subject is asked a series of two types of questions: neutral questions and critical questions. Neutral questions are those which are designed to arouse no emotion in the subject. In the case of a suspected criminal, these questions would not be related to the crime. They might be simple questions that ask for factual information, such as, "What is your name?", "Where do you work?", "How tall are you?", etc. Critical questions are concerned with the crime and are designed to arouse fear or guilt feelings in the subject. While the subject is asked both types of questions, a record is made of his physiological responses. After the test, the examiner compares the responses to the neutral questions with the responses to the critical questions. If there is a marked and consistent difference in response between the two types of questions, it is assumed that the subject probably is lying. Similarly, if there is no significant difference, it is assumed the subject is telling the truth.

It should be noted, however, that the validity of lie detectors is debatable. Lie detectors are seldom used convincingly to prove or disprove guilt in a court of law. One of the problems of the test lies in the emotionality of the subject. Some individuals may be so highly aroused by taking the test that they show strong reactions to even the neutral questions. Others may show so little emotion that their responses to critical questions may record the same as those to neutral questions. Hence, lie detection tests are not always capable of detecting lies.

### 4.2.2 Theories of Emotions

Various theories have attempted to explain the experience of emotions.

William James and Carl Lange proposed that people experience physiological changes and interpret these changes as emotions. In other words, emotions follow behavior and not vice versa. For instance, you feel afraid after you begin to perspire. (You do not perspire because you are afraid.)

**Stimulus** ⟶ **Arousal/Behavior** ⟶ **Emotion**

(Snake) ⟶ (Perspiration) ⟶ (Fear)

Walter Cannon and a colleague, P. Bard, felt that the physiological changes in many emotional states were identical. Because of this, people cannot determine their emotional state only from their physiological state. The Cannon-Bard Theory argues that emotion occurs when the **thalamus** sends signals simultaneously to the cortex and to the autonomic nervous system.

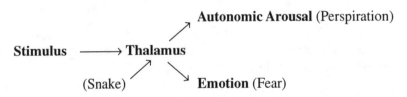

The **Common Sense Theory** argues that we **react** to emotions once they occur.

**Stimulus** ⟶ **Emotion** ⟶ **Reaction/Behavior**

(Snake) ⟶ (Fear) ⟶ (Perspiration)

Stanley Schachter's view of emotion is a **cognitive approach**. It is referred to as the **Schachter-Singer Theory**. This theory proposes that emotion occurs when physiological arousal causes us to search for reasons for this arousal. We examine the environment for an explanation for this arousal. Emotions are determined, therefore, by labeling our arousal based on what is occurring in our environment.

**Physiological Arousal** ⟶ **Appraise Environment** ⟶ **Emotion**

(Perspiration) ⟶ (A snake is present) ⟶ (Fear of snake)

or

(Perspiration) ⟶ (I'm on a date) ⟶ (I'm in love)

The **facial feedback theory** proposes that involuntary movements of the face send feedback to the brain about which emotion is being felt. This theory proposes that people universally show the same expressions when experiencing the same emotions. Five different universal facial expressions were suggested and include **happiness**, **anger**, **disgust**, **sadness**, and **fear-surprise**. For instance,

**Facial expression** ⟶ **Emotion**

(Smiling) ⟶ (Happy)

**Robert Plutchik** proposed that emotions evolved because they help a species to survive. He felt that emotions are:

**inherited** behavioral patterns, and

**modified** by experience.

According to Plutchik, there are eight **primary emotions**: **sadness**, **fear**, **surprise**, **anger**, **disgust**, **anticipation**, **joy**, and **acceptance**. Other emotions are **secondary** (or composites of primary emotions). For instance,

Surprise + Sadness = Disappointment

Fear + Acceptance = Submission

Plutchik's theory has elements of both the Common Sense Theory and Schachter's theory, as outlined on the following page.

| Stimulus event | → | Cognitive assessment of stimulus event | → | Primary emotion | → | Behavior in response to primary emotion |
|---|---|---|---|---|---|---|
| (Snake) | → | (You determine situation is dangerous.) | → | (You feel fear.) | → | (You run away.) |

## Problem Solving Examples:

**Q** Describe the following theories concerning the relationship between emotion and bodily states: the James-Lange theory, the Cannon-Bard or emergency theory, and cognitive theory.

**A** According to the James-Lange theory on the relationship of emotion and bodily states, the individual's perception of his physical reaction is the basis of his emotional experience. The emotional experience occurs after the bodily change and as a result of it. According to William James, if we see ourselves trembling, we are afraid, if we find ourselves crying, we are sad. There is a definite sequence of events in the production of an emotional state:

1. Perception of the situation that will produce the emotion.

2. Bodily reaction to the situation.

3. Perception of the reaction and the onset of the emotional reaction as a result.

According to the Cannon-Bard or emergency theory, bodily reactions do not cause emotional reactions; rather, the two occur simultaneously. The theory argues that the emotion-producing situation stimulates nerve cells in certain lower portions of the brain, which in turn activate the cerebral cortex and the body structures. Activity received by the cerebral cortex is felt as emotion, and activity received by the body structures causes bodily changes characteristic of the emotion. In the emergency theory, physiological states that result from lower brain area activity prepare the organism for emergency reactions to threatening, emotion-arousing situations.

The cognitive theory (Schachter and Singer, 1962) is somewhat similar to the James-Lange theory in that it considers felt emotion to be the result of the individual's interpretation of his aroused bodily state. The main idea behind the cognitive theory is that bodily states which accompany many various emotions are quite similar, and that even when these physiological states do differ, they cannot be sensed. They may seem different to us because we interpret them or have cognitions about them, and we feel the emotion that we believe to be the most appropriate to the arousing situation. The sequence of events in producing an emotional state, according to this theory, is:

1. Perception of the situation that will produce the emotion,

2. An arousal of a bodily state which is ambiguous, and

3. Interpretation and naming of the bodily state in terms of our notion of the external, arousing situation.

 List and describe three major types of emotional expression.

 The three major types of emotional expression are: the startle response, facial and vocal expression, and posture and gestures.

The startle response takes its name from the reaction of the subject. A startle response is usually experimentally elicited by a loud and sudden noise presented to an unsuspecting subject. The entire response occurs very quickly and has the most consistent pattern of any emotional response pattern. The response begins with a rapid closing of the eyes followed by a widening of the mouth. The head and the neck then thrust forward while the muscles of the neck stand out with the chin tilting up. Many investigators believe this to be an inborn response, thus requiring little learning or experience.

Facial and vocal expressions are much less consistent than the startle response. There is wide variety in the facial and vocal reactions of different individuals to the same stimulus. However, there are three different dimensions of emotional expression that can be observed. These are pleasantness – unpleasantness, attention – rejection, and sleep – tension. In pleasant emotions, generally, the eyes and mouth slant upward; in unpleasantness both slant downward. On the second dimension, attention is characterized by wide-open eyes, and often by flared nostrils and open mouth, while in rejection, eyes, nostrils, and mouth are all tightly shut. In sleep, for the most part, there is no facial expression and the eyes are closed. At the other extreme, tension, there is a great deal of emotional expression in the face.

The voice is also an important instrument for indicating emotion. In general, laughter indicates enjoyment; sobbing indicates sorrow; screaming can express fear or surprise; and groans denote pain or unhappiness. A low voice or a break or tremor may indicate deep sorrow. Anger is usually expressed by a sharp, loud, high-pitched voice.

Posture and gestures are the third important means of emotional expression. In happiness or pleasantness, the head is usually held high and the chest out; in sorrow, posture is often slumped with the face tilting downward; in anger, aggressive gestures are often made such as fist clenching; and in fear, the individual either flees or remains frozen in one spot.

# CHAPTER 5

# Abnormal Behavior

## 5.1 Defining Psychological Disorders

This chapter describes how psychological disorders are defined and diagnosed and presents explanations of their possible causes.

Because it is often difficult to distinguish normal from abnormal behavior, there have been several approaches for defining **abnormal behavior**. None of the definitions presented, however, is broad enough to cover all instances of abnormal or psychological disorders.

| | |
|---|---|
| **Deviation from Average (Statistical Approach)** | A statistical definition. Behaviors that are infrequent or rare are considered abnormal. The problem is that not all rare behaviors (e.g., genius) are abnormal. |
| **Deviation from Ideal (Valuative Approach)** | Considers standard behavior or what most people do. Abnormal behavior occurs when behavior deviates from the norm or what most people do. Problems with this definition are that norms change over time and people don't always agree on what ideal behavior is. |
| **Subjective Discomfort (Personal Approach)** | Behavior is abnormal if it produces distress or anxiety in an individual. A problem with this definition is that people may be feeling no distress but may be engaging in bizarre behaviors. |

| **Inability to Function (Practical Approach)** | Inability to function effectively and adapt to the demands of society are considered symptoms of abnormal behavior according to this definition. This definition does not consider personal choice. |

**Insanity** is a legal term and indicates that a person cannot be held responsible for his or her actions because of mental illness.

## 5.2 Models of Psychopathology

Psychologists use different models to understand and explain psychological disorders. A **model** is a representation that helps to organize knowledge.

| **Medical Model (Biological Model)** | Assumes the underlying cause or **etiology** of a mental disorder has a biological basis. Views psychopathology as similar to physical illness. Medication and medical therapies are often used as treatments. |

| **Learning Model** | Abnormal behaviors are learned the same way as normal behaviors – through conditioning, reinforcements, imitation, etc. Abnormal behaviors are not considered symptoms of some underlying disease – the behaviors themselves are the problem. Treatments consist of retraining and conditioning. |

| **Psychoanalytic Model (Psychodynamic Model)** | Abnormal behaviors represent unconscious motives and conflicts. Psychoanalysis is used as treatment. |

| **Humanistic-Existential Model (Phenomenological Model)** | Abnormal behaviors occur as a result of failure to fulfill one's self-potential. Emphasizes the effects of a faulty self-image. Client-centered and Gestalt |

therapies are used to increase self-acceptance.

**Cognitive Model**    Faulty or negative thinking can cause depression or anxiety. Focus of treatment is on changing faulty, irrational, or negative thinking.

## 5.3    Diagnosing and Classifying Psychological Disorders

A number of schemes have been developed for classifying and diagnosing psychological disorders. No scheme is perfect, however, and all have been criticized.

One standard system that is used by most professionals is the **Diagnostic and Statistical Manual of Mental Disorders, Fourth Edition (DSM-IV)**, which is published by the American Psychiatric Association. DSM-IV describes more than 300 specific mental disorders. A historical overview of the DSM-IV follows.

**DSM**         Published in 1952 according to a format that had been used by the army during World War II.

**DSM-II**      In 1980 the DSM was revised to conform with different classifications used by the World Health Organization.

**DSM-III**     A 1980 revision that described mental disorders in greater detail.

**DSM-III-R**   A revision of the third edition that was published in 1987, which clarified and updated the previous revision.

**DSM-IV**      The latest edition, published in 1994.

**DSM-IV** evaluates each individual according to five dimensions or axes and is therefore considered a multiaxial system of classification.

**Axis I**  Describes any mental disorder or clinical syndrome that might be present.

**Axis II**  Describes any personality disorder that might be present.

**Axis III**  Describes any physical or medical disorders that might be present.

**Axis IV**  Psychosocial and environmental problems.

**Axis V**  Assesses level of adaptive functioning currently and during the past year.

The major categories of mental disorders described in DSM-IV are described in the remaining sections of this chapter.

## Problem Solving Example:

Behavior disorders are commonly classified by professionals according to categories defined by the American Psychiatric Association. What are some criticisms of this classification system?

The American Psychiatric Association (APA) has developed a classification system of mental illnesses known as the Diagnostic and Statistical Manual (DSM). The most recent version is the DSM-IV. The classification system has been criticized on the grounds that:

(1) the diagnostic classes are not homogeneous,

(2) the system is not reliable, and

(3) the system lacks validity.

Whenever a class is formed, the behavior of all its members should be similar along the dimensions distinguishing the classification. That is, there should be some behavioral homogeneity. For example, one of the defining characteristics of an obsessive-compulsive are the intrusive thoughts which the patient seems unable to control. If we were to examine a group of people who had been classified as obsessive-compulsives, we would expect them to all display the symptom of intrusive thoughts. However, many studies have found that knowing what diagnostic category a patient falls into tells relatively little about the actual behavior of the patient. It is commonly found that certain symptoms appear in a number of diagnostic categories, thus making it difficult to predict reliably what the diagnosis will be given the occurrence of a symptom. The problem is that the current diagnostic system does not adequately specify how many of these various symptoms must be present or the degree to which they must be manifest in order to make a diagnosis. The second criticism refers to the reliability of the classification (diagnostic) system. Whether or not different diagnosticians will agree that a given diagnostic label should be applied to a particular person is the test of reliability. For a classification system to work, those applying it must be able to agree on what is and what is not an instance of a particular class. There are 3 major reasons why diagnosticians do not always agree:

(1) inconsistencies on the part of the patient, such as giving certain information to one diagnostician and not to another,

(2) inconsistencies on the part of the diagnostician, such as differences in interview techniques and interpretation of the symptoms, and

(3) inadequacies of the diagnostic system, such as unclear criteria. Either too fine a distinction was required or the system forced the diagnostician to choose a category that was not specific enough. In diagnosing abnormal behavior, no infallible measurement device exists; the only means of assessing reliability is whether or not diagnosticians agree.

The third criticism of the classification system is its lack of validity. Whether or not predictions (or valid statements) can be made about a class once it has been formed is the test of validity. Validity has a very specific relation to reliability: the less reliable a category is, the more difficult it is to make valid statements about the category. Since reliability of the current diagnostic system is not entirely adequate, by definition, we can expect that its validity will not be adequate either.

## 5.4 Anxiety Disorders

*Description.* Intense feelings of apprehension and anxiety that impede daily functioning. Approximately 8-15% of adults in this country are affected by anxiety disorders.

*Types.* Different types of anxiety disorders include:

| | |
|---|---|
| **Generalized Anxiety Disorders** | Characterized by continuous, long-lasting uneasiness and tension. Person usually cannot identify a specific cause. |
| **Panic Disorders** | Recurrent attacks of overwhelming anxiety that include heart palpitations, shortness of breath, sweating, faintness, and great fear. Often referred to as **panic attacks**. |
| **Phobic Disorders** | Intense, irrational fears of specific objects or situations. Common phobias include fears of snakes, insects, spiders, and mice/rats. **Agoraphobia** is the fear of being in public places (or away from home) and is often associated with panic disorders. |
| **Obsessive-Compulsive Disorders** | **Obsessions** are persistent, unwanted thoughts that are unreasonable (e.g., worry over germs). **Compulsions** are repetitive behaviors or mental acts performed according to certain rules or rituals (e.g., repetitive counting or checking). These behaviors or mental acts are aimed at preventing or reducing the anxiety and worry involved in the obsessions. |

*Causes.* No one theory or model adequately explains all cases of anxiety disorders. **Genetic factors** play a role; if one identical twin has a panic disorder, for example, there is a 30% chance that the other twin will have it also. **Chemical deficiencies** in the brain (low levels of certain **neurotransmitters**) and an overreaction to **lactic acid** may produce some kinds of anxiety disorder, especially obsessive-compulsive disorder. Anxiety can also be a **learned response** to stress. These disorders can also be inappropriate and inaccurate **cognitions** about one's world.

## Problem Solving Example:

 Discuss three contrasting explanations of the phenomenon of anxiety.

Anxiety is construed in different ways by different theorists. The classical psychoanalytic theory of neurotic anxiety is concerned with overstimulation (overstimulation refers to the existence of many impulses, wishes, and needs that cannot be gratified), learning theorists use a stimulus-response explanation, and other theorists utilize the concepts of control and helplessness.

Freud classical (psychoanalytic theory) based his final theory of anxiety on the idea that anxiety becomes a signal of future overstimulation. If overstimulation (by id impulses, for example) is allowed to occur, the person may be reduced to a state of extreme helplessness as at birth (which is the prototypical anxiety situation). Anxiety thus signals the ego to act prior to overstimulation.

Neurotic anxiety is the fear of the consequences of allowing a previously punished impulse to be expressed. As an example, a child develops neurotic anxiety when he or she has begun to associate punishment with the satisfaction of a particular wishful impulse. Neurotic anxiety accompanies the continued desire for gratification of this impulse. This kind of anxiety is related to a fear of the loss of love; the child imagines that gratification of a particular impulse will not only yield punishment but loss of love as well. Neurotic anxiety differs somewhat from the kind of anxiety that signals overstimulation.

Behaviorists consider anxiety to be an internal response that may be learned through classical conditioning. A tone, followed by a shock, can be shown to produce fear in rats even when the shock is subsequently taken away. Fear (or anxiety) in this stimulus-response analysis is both an internal response and a drive (which is related to avoidance behavior). However, this type of analysis has not been shown to be useful in dealing with anxious people. Since anxiety is a psychological construct and is not clearly identifiable with any set of behaviors, behaviorists are at a loss to explain it adequately. Many behaviorists reject the concept of anxiety altogether and prefer instead to discuss behavioral manifestations of "internal responses." In fact, B. F. Skinner denies that consideration of "internal responses" has any use and suggests that we should only consider overt behaviors when analyzing "behavioral problems."

One common thread in the psychoanalytic and learning theories of anxiety is the issue of control. The ego cannot control the threat of overstimulation, and the rat cannot control the painful stimulus. Experimental evidence with both humans and animals has demonstrated the importance of feelings of control or helplessness in the development of anxiety. A lack of control, or a perceived lack of control of a particular situation may lead to anxiety.

## 5.5   Somatoform Disorders

*Description.* Patterns of behavior characterized by complaints of physical symptoms in the absence of any real physical illness. About 1 person in 300 has a somatoform disorder, and they are slightly more common in women than in men.

*Types.* Hypochondriasis and conversion disorder are the two main types of somatoform disorders.

**Hypochondriasis**                     Involves a constant fear of illness, and normal aches and pains are misinterpreted as signs of disease.

**Conversion Disorder**     Unexplained symptoms or deficits affecting voluntary motor or sensory functions
that suggest a neurological or other general
medical condition. Psychological factors
are judged to be associated with the symptoms or deficits. Numbness or paralysis,
such as **glove anesthesia**, for example.

*Cause.* Conversion disorders seem to occur when an individual is
under some kind of stress. The physical condition allows the person to
escape or reduce the source of this stress.

## Problem Solving Example:

 What is a conversion reaction? What are the psychoanalytic
and behavioral theories explaining this disorder?

In conversion reactions the operations of the musculature or
sensory functions are impaired, although the bodily organs
themselves are sound. Patients with conversion disorders have reported
symptoms such as paralysis, blindness, seizures, coordination disturbance, and anesthesia, all without any sign of physiological cause. Although there are no physiological causes for the symptoms, in
conversion reaction the symptoms are not under the patient's voluntary
control.

According to psychoanalytic theory, conversion reactions are rooted
in an early unresolved Oedipus (or Electra) complex. The young child
becomes incestuously attached to the parent of the opposite sex, but
these early impulses are repressed, producing a preoccupation with sex
and, at the same time, an avoidance of it. At a later period in the
individual's life, sexual excitement or some other event reawakens these
repressed impulses, at which time they are converted into physical symptoms that represent in distorted form the repressed libidinal urges.

Ullmann and Krasner (1969) have proposed a behavioral explanation of the development of conversion reactions. In this explanation,

the person with a conversion reaction attempts to behave according to his own conception of how a person with a disease affecting his motor or sensory abilities would act. There are two conditions that increase the probability that motor and sensory disabilities can be imitated:

(1) The individual must have some experience with the role he is to adopt. He may have had similar physical problems himself, or he may have observed them in others.

(2) The enactment of the role must be rewarded. The individual's disability must result in a reduction of stress or in attainment of some positive consequence.

## 5.6 Mood Disorders

*Description.* **Mood disorders** involve moods or emotions that are extreme and unwarranted. These disturbances in emotional feelings are strong enough to intrude on everyday living.

*Types.* The most serious types of mood disorders are major depression and bipolar disorders.

**Major Depression** — Characterized by frequent episodes of intense hopelessness, lowered self-esteem, problems concentrating and making decisions, changes in eating and sleeping patterns, fatigue, reduced sex drive, and thoughts of death. Most occur for at least a two week period. Occurs twice as frequently among females as males. Can occur at any time during the life cycle; an estimated 10 – 25% of all American women will suffer from major depression at least once in their lifetime. An estimated 5 – 12% of American men will suffer from major depression at least once in their lifetime. Approximately one-half of people who attempt suicide are depressed.

| | |
|---|---|
| **Dysthymic Disorder** | More common and less severe than major depression. Similar symptoms as major depression, but they are less intense and last for a longer period (at least two years). |
| **Seasonal Affective Disorder (SAD)** | Depressive symptoms occur during the winter months when the periods of daylight are shorter. Usually crave extra sleep and eat more carbohydrates. |
| **Bipolar I Disorder** | Characterized by two emotional extremes – depression and mania. **Mania** is an elated, very active emotional state. Manic episodes alternate every few days, weeks, or years with periods of deep depression. Sometimes mood swings and behavior are severe enough to be classified as psychosis. |
| **Bipolar II Disorder** | Also characterized by extreme mood swings. Episodes include depression and at least one episode of **hypomania** (mania that is not severe enough to interfere with everyday life). |
| **Cyclothymia** | A slightly more common pattern of less extreme mood swings than bipolar disorder. |

*Causes.* Both psychological and biological theories have been proposed to explain the cause of mood disorders. There is evidence that both are correct.

Traditional **psychodynamic theory** states, for example, that depression is more frequent in people with strong dependency needs and represents anger or aggression turned inward at oneself.

Other theorists have related mood disorders to cognitive or learning factors. For instance, **Martin Seligman** suggested that depression results from **learned helplessness** or a state where people feel a lack of control over their lives and believe that they cannot cope or escape from stress so they give up trying and become depressed. **Aaron Beck** proposed that faulty thinking or cognitions cause depression because depressed people typically make pessimistic predictions about self, the world, and their future. **Learning theorists** propose that depression is learned through reinforcement or imitation of depressive behaviors.

Biological factors also appear to play a role in mood disorders. For instance, there is evidence that depression can be caused by a **chemical imbalance** in the brain because the **norepinephrine** and **serotonin** systems are malfunctioning. The cyclical nature of many mood disorders suggests that abnormalities in **biological rhythms** and **genetics** may play a role too. This appears especially true for bipolar disorder. For example, if one member of an identical-twin pair develops bipolar disorder, 72% of the other members usually develop the disorder. Children with depressed parents are also more likely to develop depression.

## Problem Solving Example:

Describe the two major physiological theories of depression.

These are two major theories concerning what physiological processes may be disrupted to bring on depression. Both theories implicate biochemical factors. The first theory is concerned primarily with electrolyte metabolism and the second with the chemicals involved in neural transmission.

Electrolytes dissolve and dissociate into electrically charged moving particles which carry electric current. Two of the most important electrolytes are sodium and potassium chlorides. The positively charged sodium and potassium particles are distributed differently on either side of the membrane of a nerve cell. There is a higher concentration of sodium outside the neuron and a higher concentration of potassium within it. This difference helps maintain what is referred to as the "resting potential" of the cell. Alterations in the distribution of sodium and potassium produce changes in the resting potential, which in turn affect the excitability of the neuron, that is, whether it is readily excited and thus fired by impulses transmitted from another neuron.

A second, more modern, physiological theory of mood disorders suggests that depression may arise from disruptions in the delicate balance of neurotransmitters (the substances that regulate and mediate the activity of the brain's nerve cells, or neurons). Neurotransmitters, released by the activated presynaptic neuron, mediate the transfer of nerve impulses from one nerve to the next in the neural pathway. Neurotransmitters may either stimulate or inhibit the firing of the next neuron in the chain. Early research efforts identified deficits in two neurotransmitters, norepinephrine and serotonin, as being linked to depression. More recent research indicates that the link between neurotransmitters and depression is not as straightforward as initially hypothesized.

## 5.7   Dissociative Disorders

*Description.* Characterized by a loss of contact with portions of consciousness or memory, resulting in disruptions in one's sense of self. They appear to be an attempt to overcome anxiety and stress by dissociating oneself from the core of one's personality and result in a loss of memory, identity, or consciousness.

*Types.* The major dissociative disorders are:

**Dissociative Amnesia**  Either partial or total memory loss that can last from a few hours to many years. Usually remembers nonthreatening aspects of life. There appears to be no physical cause but often results from stress. (That is, one "doesn't remember" stressful aspects of one's life.)

**Dissociative Fugue**  People suddenly leave or "flee" their present life and establish a new, different existence and identity in a new location. Their former life is blocked from memory. Often they return from their fugue state to their former life just as suddenly as they left.

| | |
|---|---|
| **Dissociative Identity Disorder** | One person develops two or more distinct identities or personality states. |

*Cause.* Dissociative disorders allow people to escape from an anxiety producing situation. The person either produces a new personality to deal with the stress, or the situation that caused the stress is forgotten or left behind. For instance, researchers have found that about 94% of people with Dissociative Identity Disorder were abused as children. Not all abused children, however, exhibit multiple identities or personality states.

## Problem Solving Example:

 What are the psychoanalytic and behavioral theories of dissociative disorders?

In dissociative reactions a group of mental processes splits off from the mainstream of consciousness, or behavior becomes incompatible with the rest of the personality. The psychoanalytic and behavioral accounts of dissociative disorders are not dissimilar, although each stresses different concepts.

In psychoanalytic theory, dissociative reactions are viewed as instances of massive repression of unacceptable urges, usually relating back to the infantile sexual wishes of the Oedipal stage. In adulthood these Oedipal yearnings increase in strength until they are finally expressed, usually as an impulsive sexual act. The expression of these unacceptable urges means that the defenses against them have failed totally; consequently, a new defense is needed. The unacceptable urges and the stressful event in which they found expression have to be obliterated from consciousness. To do this, the person segments an entire part of the personality from awareness.

Behavioral theory also construes dissociative reactions as an attempt to protect the individual from stress; however, in this theory the concept of repression is not employed and the importance of infantile sexual conflicts is not accepted. Rather, dissociative reactions are viewed simply as an avoidance response used by the individual to escape stressful stimuli.

## 5.8   Personality Disorders

*Description.* **Personality disorders** are patterns of traits that are long-standing, maladaptive, and inflexible and keep a person from functioning properly in society. Behavior often disrupts social relationships. Personality disorders are coded on **Axis II** of the **DSM-IV** system for diagnosing mental disorders.

*Types.* Representative types of personality disorders are described below.

**Antisocial**      Displays no regard for moral or ethical rules and continuously violates the rights of others. Is manipulative, impulsive, and lacks feelings for others. Also appears to lack a conscience or guilt.

**Narcissistic**    An exaggerated sense of self and self-importance; preoccupied with fantasies of success. Lacks empathy. Often expects special treatment.

**Paranoid**        Continual unjustified suspicion and mistrust of people. Often appears cold and unemotional. Easily offended.

**Histrionic**      Overreacts and overdramatic in response to minor situations. Often seen as vain, shallow, dependent, or manipulative.

**Avoidant**        Tends to be a "loner," or social snob. Oversensitive to rejection or possible humiliation. Has low self-esteem.

**Schizotypal**     Strangeness in thinking, speech, and behavior. Cognitive and perceptual disturbances.

| Schizoid | Acute discomfort from social relationships. Restricted range of emotional expression. |
| Borderline | Instability in interpersonal relationships, self-image, and affect. Marked impulsivity. |
| Dependent | Pattern of submissive and clinging behavior related to an excessive need to be taken care of. |
| Obsessive-Compulsive | Preoccupation with orderliness, perfectionism, and control. |

*Causes.* Suggested causes for personality disorders range from problems in family relationships to a biological inability to experience emotions. A growing body of evidence indicates that biological problems may be the cause of many personality disorders.

## Problem Solving Example:

**Q** What are the symptoms of a delusional disorder? Discuss the different types of this disorder.

**A** The essential features of a delusional disorder are persistent, nonbizarre delusions of at least one month's duration. Apart from the impact of the delusions, people suffering from this disorder are not markedly impaired and their behavior is not obviously odd or bizarre. Delusional disorders follow particular themes and are subclassified in the following categories:

| Erotomanic Type | Delusions that another person, usually of higher status, is romantically interested in the individual. |
| Grandiose Type | Delusions of special powers, exceptional knowledge or skills, inflated worth or identity, or special relationship with famous or powerful people. |
| Jealous Type | Delusions that one's sexual partner is having an affair. |

| | |
|---|---|
| **Persecutory Type** | Delusions that either they or a loved one is being persecuted in some way. |
| **Somatic Type** | Delusions that the person has some medical condition or physical defect. |
| **Mixed Type** | Delusional characteristics that combine the above types with no predominant theme. |
| **Unspecified Type** | Does not fit any of the previous categories. |

Paranoid disorder differs from paranoid schizophrenia and paranoid personality. The distinction among these disorders is vague. Generally, a paranoid disorder involves less loss of contact with reality than is seen in paranoid schizophrenia and more loss of contact with reality than is seen in paranoid personality disorders.

## 5.9  Schizophrenic Disorders

*Description*. **Schizophrenia** is a serious **psychotic disorder** (i.e., one is out-of-touch with reality). Schizophrenia is **NOT** the same as multiple personality disorder, although this is a common misperception. Schizophrenia involves **disorders of thought**. Schizophrenics display problems in both how they think and what they think.

Schizophrenic thinking is often **incoherent**. For instance, they sometimes use **neologisms** or words that only have meaning to the person speaking them (e.g., the word "glump"). **Loose associations**, where thought appears logically unconnected, is another characteristic that is sometimes seen. **Word salad** describes a jumble of words that are spoken that do not make sense.

The **content** of a schizophrenic's thinking is also disturbed. Various kinds of delusions are common. **Delusions** are false beliefs that are maintained even though they are clearly out of touch with reality. Common delusions are beliefs that they are being controlled by someone else, that someone is out to get them, that they are a famous person from history (e.g., the President of the United States), and that their thoughts are being broadcast so that others are able to know what they are thinking.

A person with schizophrenia may also experience **hallucinations** or the experience of perceiving things that do not actually exist. The most common hallucination is hearing voices that do not exist.

Schizophrenics also tend to display **flat** (absent) or **inappropriate affect**. Even dramatic events tend to produce little or no emotional reaction from a schizophrenic. The emotional responses they do display often are bizarre and unexpected.

A person with schizophrenia usually has little interest in others and appears **socially withdrawn.**

**Abnormal motor behavior** may also occur, such as unusual pacing back and forth, rocking constantly, or being immobilized for long periods of time.

Schizophrenia usually involves a noticeable **deterioration in functioning**. That is, the person used to function adaptively (and did not display symptoms of schizophrenia) but now the quality of work, social relations, and personal care have deteriorated. Their previous level of functioning has broken down.

*Types.* Five major subtypes of schizophrenia are described in DSM-IV.

| | |
|---|---|
| **Disorganized** | Severe deterioration of adaptive behavior. Speech incoherent. Strange facial grimaces common. Inappropriate silliness, babbling, giggling, and obscene behavior may be displayed. Includes 5% of schizophrenics. |
| **Catatonic** | Characterized by disordered movement. Alternates between extreme withdrawal where the body is kept very still and extreme excitement where movement is rapid and speech incoherent. **Waxy flexibility** describes the odd posturing. Makes up about 8% of all cases. |

**Paranoid**                    Delusions of persecution or grandeur. Judgment
                                is impaired and unpredictable. Often includes
                                anxiety, anger, jealousy, or argumentativeness.
                                Hallucinations are common. Tends to appear
                                later in life than the other types. Onset is often
                                sudden. Less impaired. Makes up about 40%
                                of all schizophrenics.

**Undifferentiated**            No one subtype dominates. About 40% of all
                                schizophrenics receive this diagnosis.

**Residual**                    Has had a prior episode of schizophrenia but
                                currently is not displaying major symptoms.
                                Subtle indications of schizophrenia may be ob-
                                served, however.

*Causes.* Genetic, biological, psychological, and environmental factors have been used to explain the origin of schizophrenia. No one theory,
however, can adequately account for all forms of schizophrenia.

Twin studies have suggested a **hereditary** or **genetic** component
to schizophrenia. When one identical twin is identified as schizophrenic,
the other twin has a 42 – 48% chance of also developing schizophrenia. Children of schizophrenics who are adopted by nonschizophrenics
also have a higher incidence of schizophrenia than control populations.
Schizophrenia, therefore, does run in families.

Most people with schizophrenic relatives, however, do not develop
schizophrenia. This has led researchers to conclude that what might be
inherited is a **predisposition** or genetic **vulnerability** for schizophrenia. What is needed for schizophrenia to develop is this genetic predisposition plus environmental stress. This is often referred to as the
**predisposition** or **vulnerability model** and the **diathesis-stress model**.

**Neurochemical factors** are also related to schizophrenia. Schizophrenia appears to be accompanied by changes in the activity of one or
more **neurotransmitters** in the brain. The **dopamine hypothesis** suggests that schizophrenia occurs when there is excess activity in those

areas of the brain using dopamine to transmit nerve impulses. Excessive dopamine appears related to delusions.

Some researchers have suggested that **structural abnormalities in the brain** are linked to schizophrenia. Studies have suggested that schizophrenic individuals have difficulty focusing their attention and display bizarre behaviors because of brain abnormalities. Such structural abnormalities might include shrinking or deterioration of cells in the cerebral cortex that cause enlargements of the brain's fluid-filled ventricles, reduced blood flow in parts of the brain, and abnormalities in **brain lateralization** or in the ways the hemispheres of the brain communicate with each other.

**Psychoanalytic theorists** propose that schizophrenia represents a regression to earlier stages in life when the id was the most dominant aspect of personality.

Other theorists assert that schizophrenia is a learned behavior and consists of a set of inappropriate responses to social stimuli. This is sometimes referred to as the **learned-inattention theory**. Defective or faulty communication patterns within the family may also be learned and therefore result in schizophrenia. Such faulty communication might include unintelligible speech, stories with no ending, extensive contradictions, and poor attention to child's attempts at communicating.

The **two-strike theory** suggests a prenatal link to schizophrenia. According to this theory, the **first strike** is an inherited susceptibility of the fetal brain to be disrupted by exposure to the flu virus during the second trimester of pregnancy. The **second strike** occurs when exposure to the flu virus actually occurs during the second trimester of pregnancy. Microscopic examination of the brains of schizophrenics does indicate that whatever is going wrong in their brains probably occurred during the second trimester of pregnancy.

It appears, therefore, that schizophrenia is associated with several possible causes. Schizophrenia is probably not caused by a single factor but by a combination of interrelated variables.

## Problem Solving Examples:

**Q**     What are the features of schizophrenic behavior?

**A**     The disordered behavior of schizophrenic patients can be organized into disturbances in several major areas – cognition, perception and attention, affect or emotion, motor behavior, and contact with reality. Usually a patient diagnosed as schizophrenic will exhibit only some of these disturbances. The diagnostician must decide how many problems must be present, and in what degree, to justify the diagnosis of schizophrenia.

Disorders of cognition include thought disorders and delusions. Thought disorder is a behavior that is absolutely essential to a schizophrenic diagnosis. Disturbances in a schizophrenic's thought processes are manifested in his verbal behavior. Usually a schizophrenic will speak incoherently, making references to ideas or images that are not connected. Often he will use neologisms (words made up by the speaker). Thought may also be disordered by loose associations. The individual may have difficulty sticking to one topic, often drifting off on a series of idiosyncratic associations. Another aspect of the schizophrenic's associative problems is the use of clang associations. The patient's speech contains many words associated only by rhyme; for example, "How are you in your shoe on a pew, Doctor?" The words follow one another because they rhyme, not because they make logical sense.

Delusions, another type of cognitive disorder, are beliefs contrary to reality that are firmly held in spite of contradictory evidence. Typically, schizophrenics have delusions of persecution, grandeur, or control. A person with delusions of persecution believes that others are plotting against him. With delusions of grandeur the person believes that he is an especially important individual, such as a famous movie star or Christ reincarnate. Delusions of control involve the person's believing that he is being controlled by some outside force, such as alien beings or radar waves. Delusions may be transient or systematized – systematized delusions are highly organized delusions that become the dominant focus of a person's life.

Disorders of perception and attention are often evident in the reports of schizophrenic patients. Some mention changes in the way their bodies feel. Parts of their bodies may seem too large or too small, or there may be numbness or tingling. Some schizophrenics remark that the world appears flat or colorless. The most dramatic distortions of perception are called hallucinations, sensory experiences in the absence of any relevant stimulation from the environment. The hallucinations of schizophrenics are not the meaningless patterns of colors and sounds such as may occur during a drug experience. Rather, schizophrenics may hear voices or music, or they may see unreal people or objects. In addition, schizophrenics often have trouble attending to what is happening around them. For example, a schizophrenic may be unable to concentrate on television because he cannot watch the screen and listen to what is being said at the same time.

Three affective abnormalities are often found in schizophrenic patients. In some, affect may be flat; that is, virtually no stimulus can elicit an emotional response. Other patients display inappropriate affect. The emotional responses of these individuals do not fit the situation. The patient may laugh upon hearing that his mother has just died, or he may become enraged when asked a simple question like how he feels. Finally, the affective responses of some schizophrenic patients are ambivalent. A single person or object may simultaneously arouse both positive and negative emotions. A patient may express strong hatred and strong love toward another person at about the same time.

The motor symptoms of schizophrenia are obvious and somewhat bizarre. The schizophrenic may grimace or adopt strange facial expressions. The overall level of activity may be increased, the patient may exhibit much excitement and expend great amounts of energy by running around and flailing his limbs wildly. At the other end of the spectrum these may be catatonic immobility – unusual postures are adopted and maintained for very long periods of time.

Most schizophrenics have little or no grasp of reality. They tend to withdraw from contact with the world into their own thoughts and fantasies. Usually a schizophrenic becomes unable to distinguish between his own fictitious constructions of reality and what is really happening.

Briefly discuss the following types of schizophrenia: catatonic, paranoid, disorganized, undifferentiated, and residual.

Because of the wide variety of symptoms associated with schizophrenia, psychologists have found it helpful for diagnostic and treatment purposes to distinguish among different types of schizophrenia. Classification of a schizophrenic into one or another of the subtypes depends upon how the psychosis developed and/or upon what kinds of symptoms are predominant in the patient's behavior. It is rare to find a schizophrenic who fits neatly into one of the subcategories of schizophrenia. This discussion will cover the types of schizophrenia listed in DSM-IV.

Disturbances in motor functions are the most obvious symptoms of the catatonic type of schizophrenia. A catatonic schizophrenic typically alternates between immobility and wild excitement, but often one or the other type of motor symptoms may predominate. In the excited state the catatonic may shout and talk continuously and incoherently, all the while pacing back and forth. The immobile state is characterized by physical rigidity, muteness, and unresponsiveness. Despite the severity of its symptoms, catatonia is more likely than other forms of schizophrenia to "cure itself" without treatment.

The paranoid schizophrenic is characterized by the presence of numerous and systematized delusions, usually of persecution, but sometimes of grandeur or of being controlled by an alien force. Auditory and visual hallucinations may accompany the delusions. Generally, paranoid schizophrenics are more alert and verbal than other schizophrenics. They tend to intellectualize, building up an organized set of beliefs based on the wrong assumptions. Their thought processes, although deluded, are not as fragmented as those of other schizophrenics.

The disorganized (or hebephrenic) schizophrenic displays a variety of bizarre symptoms. Hallucinations and delusions are profuse and very poorly organized. They typically exhibit severe regression to childhood behavior which is marked by a pattern of silliness and absurdity. They may grimace or giggle wildly for no reason, or they may speak incoherently, stringing together similar-sounding words and making up words of their own. They often completely neglect their appearance, never bathing or combing their hair, and often they will deteriorate to the point that they become incontinent, voiding anywhere and anytime.

The label undifferentiated is applied to those schizophrenics who do not exhibit a pattern of symptoms consistent enough to fit one of the other subtypes. For example, a patient may have highly organized delusions or motor disorders, but not to the extent that he is considered either a paranoid or a catatonic schizophrenic. This particular category has been criticized as being somewhat of a "wastebasket diagnosis" which is applied simply because a patient is difficult to categorize. The patient is, to put it simply, "very crazy," but not in any systematic manner.

The diagnosis of residual schizophrenia is applied to a patient who has had an episode of schizophrenic illness but does not now exhibit any psychotic symptoms, although non-psychotic signs of the illness persist. Emotional blunting, social withdrawal, and communication disorder are common in residual schizophrenics.

**Q** Citing specific investigations, discuss what the results of twin studies have suggested about the role of heredity in the development of schizophrenia.

**A** Concordance is the similarity in psychiatric diagnosis or other traits in a pair of twins. To research the role of genetic factors in schizophrenia, twin studies were designed to find out whether the concordance rate for schizophrenia is greater for identical (monozygotic) twins, than it is for fraternal (dizygotic) twins.

In a major study in Norway, Kringlen (1967) found a 38 percent concordance for identical twins as contrasted with 10 percent in fraternal twins. There were 55 pairs of identical twins and 172 pairs of fraternal twins. Gottesman and Shields (1972) found a concordance rate of 42 percent for identical (MZ) and 9 percent for fraternal twins (DZ) who were hospitalized and diagnosed as schizophrenic. They also found that the concordance was much higher for twins with severe schizophrenic disorders than for those with mild symptoms. A review conducted in 1994 of the worldwide literature on twin studies in schizophrenia concluded that the overall pairwise concordance rate for MZ twins is 28 percent.

Although the concordance rate for schizophrenia in identical twins is high, the discordance rate is higher. If schizophrenia were solely the result of genetic factors, the concordance rate for identical twins would be one hundred. One must also take into account that since the twins have been reared together, a common environment rather than common genetic factors may account for concordance rates.

In a study by Rosenthal (1970), 16 pairs of monozygotic twins were reared apart from very early childhood. Of the 16 pairs, 10 were concordant and 6 were discordant. The concordance rate of this limited sample was 62.5 percent, a finding that supports the view that a predisposition for schizophrenia is genetically transmitted. Because of the small sample size, however, the data cannot be regarded as conclusive.

Although studies have not proven that schizophrenia is solely transmitted through genetic factors, the findings support the view that a predisposition for schizophrenia may exist. Here it is presumed that certain individuals are more prone to develop schizophrenia if placed under severe stress. However, given a more favorable life situation, the individuals' inherent vulnerability may never exhibit itself in the form of schizophrenic behavior.

## Quiz: Motivation and Emotion – Abnormal Behavior

1. Research suggests that people perform best when arousal is

    (A) low.

    (B) moderate.

    (C) high.

    (D) No research exists that proves a relationship between arousal and performance levels.


2. Rats with injury to the ventromedial hypothalamus

    (A) became overeaters.

    (B) stopped eating.

    (C) stopped gaining weight.

    (D) None of the above.


3. The _____ argues that emotion occurs when the thalamus sends signals simultaneously to the cortex and to the autonomic nervous system.

    (A) The Cannon-Bard Theory

    (B) The Common Sense Theory

    (C) Schachter-Singer Theory

    (D) Facial Feedback Theory

4.  The _____ proposes that emotion occurs when physiological arousal causes us to search for reasons for this arousal.

    (A)  The Cannon-Bard Theory

    (B)  The Common Sense Theory

    (C)  Schachter-Singer Theory

    (D)  Facial Feedback Theory

5.  According to Plutchik, all of the following are primary emotions EXCEPT

    (A)  surprise.

    (B)  sadness.

    (C)  disgust.

    (D)  disappointment.

6.  Another name for the valuative approach, in regards to psychological disorders, is

    (A)  deviation from average.

    (B)  deviation from ideal.

    (C)  subjective discomfort.

    (D)  inability to function.

7.  The focus of the _____ model is that faulty or negative thinking causes depression or anxiety.

    (A)  psychoanalytical

    (B)  humanistic-existential

(C)  cognitive

(D)  medical

8.   Glove anesthesia is an example of a(n)

(A)  conversion disorder.

(B)  panic disorder.

(C)  phobic disorder.

(C)  obsessive-compulsive disorder.

9.   There is evidence that depression can be caused by chemical imbalance in the brain because of malfunction related to which neurotransmitter(s)?

(A)  Norepinephrine

(B)  Serotonin

(C)  Both (A) and (B).

(D)  None of the above

10.   _____ is a disorder in which people suddenly "flee" their present life and establish a new identity in a new location with no recollection of their former life. Often, they return from this state to their former life as suddenly as they left.

(A)  Paranoia

(B)  Multiple personalities

(C)  Psychogenic amnesia

(D)  Dissociative fugue

## ANSWER KEY

1. (B)
2. (A)
3. (A)
4. (C)
5. (D)

6. (B)
7. (C)
8. (A)
9. (C)
10. (D)

# CHAPTER 6

# Psychotherapy

## 6.1 Therapy

**Psychotherapy** is the treatment of emotional and behavioral problems through psychological techniques. Psychotherapy uses psychological rather than biological approaches to treatment. Psychotherapy involves conversation or verbal interactions between a person with a psychological disorder and someone who has been trained to help correct that disorder, a **therapist**.

Historically, one early approach to treating mental illness used by Stone Age society was **trepanning** or boring a hole in the skull of the patient. Needless to say, many did not survive this primitive procedure.

During the Middle Ages, treatment focused on **demonology** or blaming supernatural forces for the mentally ill. **Exorcism** was used to drive out the evil.

Following the French Revolution in 1792, **Philippe Pinel** reformed the ways that patients were treated in mental hospitals by arguing for more humane treatments.

By the mid-1800s, many began to realize that abnormal behavior could result from damage to the brain and central nervous system. Over the years there has been an explosive growth in the number of therapies available to treat mental illness. General descriptions of the various types of therapies and therapeutic techniques that have been developed include:

**Insight Therapy**    Any psychotherapy where the goal is to help clients better understand themselves, their situation, or their problems.

**Action Therapy**    This therapy focuses on directly changing a troubling habit or behavior.

**Directive Therapy**    Any approach in which the therapist provides strong guidance during therapy sessions.

**Nondirective Therapy**    A therapeutic technique in which clients assume responsibility for solving their own problems. The therapist creates a supportive atmosphere so this can happen.

**Individual Therapy**    A therapy session involving one client and one therapist.

**Group Therapy**    A therapy session that includes several clients at one time and one or more therapists. One particular problem or difficulty is usually the focus (e.g., alcoholism or eating disorders).

**Family Therapy**    An approach that focuses on the family as a whole unit. The goal is to avoid labeling a single family member as the focus of therapy; each person's contribution to the group is the focus.

**Outpatient Therapy**    Clients receive psychotherapy while they live in the community.

**Inpatient Therapy**    Clients receive psychotherapy while in a hospital or other residential institution.

**Therapists** represent a variety of theoretical orientations and professional backgrounds. The major professionals involved in psychotherapy are described in the table that follows.

| Type | Degree | Description |
|------|--------|-------------|
| **Clinical** or **Counseling Psychologists** | Ph.D. or Psy.D. | Trained to diagnose, test, and treat individuals with psychological disorders. |
| **Psychiatrists** | M.D. | Medical doctors who specialize in treating psychological disorders. They can prescribe medication. |
| **Social Workers** | M.S.W. | Have a Masters of Social Work degree and specialize in counseling and therapy. |
| **Psychoanalysts** | M.D., Ph.D., or Psy.D. | Usually psychiatrists, but can be psychologists who are trained in in the psychoanalytic techniques of Sigmund Freud. |
| **Psychiatric Nurses** | B.S.N. or M.A./M.S. | Usually work with patients while they are hospitalized for psychiatric care. |
| **Counselors** | M.A. or M.S. | Usually provide supportive therapy, family therapy, or drug and alcohol abuse counseling. |

## Problem Solving Examples:

 What is the basic goal and logic of psychotherapy and how is this goal generally achieved?

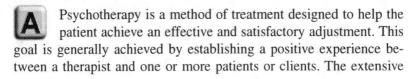 Psychotherapy is a method of treatment designed to help the patient achieve an effective and satisfactory adjustment. This goal is generally achieved by establishing a positive experience between a therapist and one or more patients or clients. The extensive

research and use of different psychotherapies has resulted in the establishing of certain conditions which are believed to be necessary for positive change. Each specific therapy (e.g., client-centered, behavior, psychoanalytic, etc.) has its own set of "strategies" which are based on therapeutic experiences and the underlying theories. In actual practice, the notion of psychotherapy is both a "contrast" between the therapist and client and a highly interpersonal relationship in which skill, empathy and concern are necessary characteristics for the therapist.

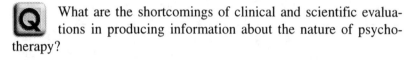 What are the shortcomings of clinical and scientific evaluations in producing information about the nature of psychotherapy?

Studies of the outcome of psychotherapy with neurotic patients have shown that about two-thirds of treated adults show marked improvement or recover within two years. These figures are consistent regardless of the type of therapy. The results are not as remarkable as they may seem because the recovery rate of untreated patients is also about 65%. In this context "treated" refers to having undergone a treatment procedure with a trained professional therapist. Many people with neurotic difficulties seek help from nonprofessionals and it appears that this nonprofessional help is about as effective as the treatment procedures used by trained specialists.

These figures may, however, be misleading due to the difficulties inherent in measuring the degree of improvement in these types of cases. A major methodological problem is matching the severity and kinds of problems presented by treated and untreated patients and by patients who have undergone different types of therapy which may use different labels or descriptions for the disorders being treated. The lack of valid, consistent criteria for evaluating improvement is another large problem. Some of the criteria that have been used are: the therapist's subjective determination, the client's self-evaluation, changes in the performance on adjustment measurement tests administered before and after therapy. The criteria that have been used in measuring changes in overt behavior include: the absence of symptoms that were formerly present, better use of potentialities, improved interpersonal relationships and improvement in attitudes.

There is evidence that untreated patients show moderate improvement over time, whereas treated patients tend to show marked improvement or a marked change for the worse. An inappropriate therapy or therapist can worsen a problem. It is becoming clearer that the therapeutic intervention selected must match the specific type of patient within a given set of circumstances. For instance, behavior therapy appears to be excellent for treating phobic reactions; highly educated, mildly disturbed neurotic patients respond best to traditional psychoanalysis. To answer the question, "Is psychotherapy effective?" one needs to consider the type of therapy and the disturbance.

## 6.2   Insight Therapies

As stated above, the goal of **insight therapies** is for clients to gain insight or increased understanding of themselves in order to promote changes in personality and behavior. There are at least 200 different insight therapies available today. The more popular ones are described in the following sections.

### 6.2.1   Traditional Psychoanalysis

**Psychoanalysis** is an insight therapy that emphasizes the understanding of unconscious conflicts, motives, and defense mechanisms. Traditional psychoanalysis was developed by **Sigmund Freud** (see chapter 2 for an overview of Freud's theory of personality).

At first Freud and his colleague **Joseph Breuer** tried to use **hypnosis** either to help patients or clients recall events from their past or to cure them by using **hypnotic suggestion**.

When hypnosis proved unsuccessful, Freud had patients relax on a couch and merely talk about their memories. This came to be known as the **talking cure**.

Freud treated people who seemed to have phobias, panic disorders, obsessive-compulsive disorders, and conversion disorders. He referred to these disorders as **neuroses**. Freud felt that neurotic disorders were caused by unconscious conflicts that were left over from early childhood. He concluded that the neurotic or **hysterical** symptoms displayed by his patients developed out of these unconscious conflicts, wishes, and fantasies from their childhoods.

The goal of traditional psychoanalysis is to help patients gain insight into their unconscious thoughts and emotions and to understand how these unconscious elements affect their everyday life. Treatment may require many sessions per week over the course of several years.

Psychoanalysts seek to maintain a **neutral relationship** with clients so the clients can reveal their unresolved unconscious conflicts. Techniques used by traditional psychoanalysts include:

**Free Association**　　Patients do not censor their thoughts or words but are encouraged to spontaneously say whatever comes to their mind. In order to encourage this, patients relax by lying on a couch, facing away from the analyst.

**Dream Analysis**　　Freud felt that dreams were "the royal road to the unconscious," whereby the id feels free to reveal itself. The **manifest content** of dreams is what the patient actually remembers about the dream. The **latent content** is what the dream symbolizes. Psychoanalysts help interpret the latent content for patients.

**Interpretations**　　Psychoanalysts offer insights or alternative ways of looking at dreams, thoughts, and behaviors based on possible unconscious needs and desires.

**Defense Mechanisms**　　Throughout therapy, analysts look for signs of possible defense mechanisms (described in chapter 2).

**Transference**  Analysts believe if they maintain a neutral relationship with patients and reveal nothing about themselves, transference will develop. Transference occurs when patients transfer feelings about other people (e.g., their parents) to their perception of their therapist. Possible signs of transference include falling in love or being hostile with the therapist.

**Resistance**  Resistance involves any unconscious behaviors by the patient that hinder the progress of therapy. Some examples include being late for therapy sessions, missing sessions, or becoming angry at the therapist.

Critics of psychoanalysis argue that treatment is expensive and requires good verbal skills on the part of the client. It is also basically untestable and difficult to measure scientifically.

## Problem Solving Examples:

**Q** What are the aims of psychoanalysis?

 **A** Operating within the framework of Freudian theory, the psychoanalyst's goal in therapy is the reconstruction of the patient's personality. To effect this reconstruction, the underlying causes for the patient's apparent maladaptive symptoms must be uncovered and explored in depth. In brief, the material of the unconscious mind needs to be brought into the conscious mind so that it no longer serves as a source of anxiety and confusion for the patient.

The psychoanalyst believes that simply curing the symptoms of a particular problem will not relieve the main difficulty for the patient; the underlying conflicting repressed impulses will simply seek expression in some other way. For this reason, it is vital to focus on the source of whatever symptoms there may be.

This type of therapy is long, intensive and usually expensive. The patient is expected to visit the analyst at least four to five times per week for one to two years for a complete analysis to take place. During this time, the psychosexual development of the individual will be retraced through free association and dream analysis. The psychoanalyst will use this information to locate the source of the current problems and to help the patient come to terms with the troublesome unconscious material. When he accomplishes this he will relieve the repression.

The analyst will then work toward the reconstruction of a new, sounder personality that will be more effective in dealing with life situations and relationships. In psychoanalytic terminology, the ego or rational, mature, conscious part of an individual is strengthened at the expense of the id or irrational, immature and unconscious aspects through a process that makes the unconscious conscious.

 Describe the basic strategy and treatment procedure of psychoanalysis.

Although psychoanalysis appears to be a constantly changing area, many of the basic contentions outlined and developed by Freud are still applicable. The basic contention of psychoanalytic theory is that all forms of psychopathology result from the repression of unacceptable drives, inner conflicts (anxieties), and defense mechanisms which reduce the anxiety but do not affect the conflict, thus giving rise to improper psychological development. Instead of dealing with inner conflicts, the patient represses the conflicts into the unconscious and is rendered helpless by his own defenses. Psychoanalytic theory then contends that these repressed inner conflicts are revealed in unconscious actions, dreams, and pathological symptoms. The basic goal of therapy therefore is to aid the patient in overcoming this resistance.

Since many conflicts are hypothesized to have been repressed during childhood, the patient often acts towards the therapist in the same ways he acted towards his parents when he was younger. The establishing of this kind of emotional tie is called "transference."

Freud developed (with Breuer) the technique of free association. In this process, the patient says anything that comes to mind and the therapist is able to direct the flow of associations to the source of the pathology. In addition to this method of freeing repressed conflicts, Freud also developed a system for interpreting dreams as a tool for "entering" the repressed areas of the patient's unconscious mind. The analytic session itself is designed to optimally maximize the occurrence of transference. The therapist, by remaining quiet and aloof, provides the patient with a "clean slate" on which to transfer the parental attributions.

The process of transference, the technique of free association, and dream interpretation all serve to give the patient meaningful insight into the conflicts that are preventing normal adjustment and corrective change.

 Define transference. Describe the interaction between patient and analyst in the transference neurosis.

One of the purposes of traditional psychoanalysis is to bring the unconscious, repressed material of the patient into consciousness. The analytic technique called "transference" figures importantly in the success of therapy. "Transference" is the name given by Freud to the tendency of the patient to react to the therapist with the same childhood emotions he used to experience toward his parents; one of the main roles of the therapist, therefore, is to serve as a transference object.

This peculiar emotional attachment to the analyst usually begins to develop during the process of "free association" – a technique whereby the patient reports whatever thoughts, feelings or images come to mind, no matter how trivial or unimportant they seem to be. Because material from the unconscious is seen as always seeking expression, this technique is thought to encourage the expression of this repressed material. Generally, the patient resists the recall of painful or guilty memories, and it is a further role of the analyst to help the patient overcome this resistance. In expressing and reliving his past, the patient transfers to the analyst the hostilities, affections, resentment and guilt he formerly felt toward his parents. Thus, transference brings the problems into the open where they can be analyzed in a rational manner.

These displaced and often intense and inappropriate reactions of the patient to the analyst are referred to as "transference neurosis." It is through the interpretation and examination of this neurosis that the patient learns that his childish reactions are no longer appropriate within the adult world. This frees the individual from childhood fixations and makes available large amounts of energy that were formerly used in repressing the unconscious material.

The resolution of the transference neurosis is one of the most important parts of the cure in classical psychoanalysis. For it to occur successfully, the analyst must be able to maintain the stance of compassionate neutrality. His role is mainly to listen and offer interpretations. He must guard against letting his own personality intrude upon the patient's working out of his problems. It is partly for this reason that all doctors trained as psychoanalysts must undergo psychoanalytic treatment themselves before they begin to practice.

## 6.2.2 Modern Psychoanalysis

The term **psychodynamic** is often used to refer to a variety of approaches that descended from Freud's theory and were developed by **neo-Freudians** (see chapter 2). Examples include **ego analysis, interpersonal therapy, individual analysis**, and **object relations therapy**.

Psychodynamic therapies differ from traditional psychoanalysis in several important ways:

- Most do not use the Freudian "couch" but rather sit face-to-face with their patients.

- They explore conscious thoughts and feelings as much as unconscious ones and, therefore, focus on current problems as well as childhood conflicts.

- They emphasize the concept of working through or developing new behaviors and emotions following insight.

- Their therapy is often more streamlined – does not require as many sessions per week nor as many total sessions and is, therefore, often less expensive.

- Some therapists have developed techniques to use with children.

### 6.2.3 Humanistic Therapies

Humanistic therapies (sometimes called **phenomenological**) are also insight-oriented therapies. The humanist view is optimistic and the emphasis of therapy is on fulfilling one's potential. Client-Centered, Gestalt, and Existential are forms of humanistic therapy.

**Carl Rogers** founded **client-centered** or **person-centered therapy**. This therapy attempts to focus on the person's own point of view, instead of the therapist's interpretations. The client or person, therefore, is the center of the process and determines what will be discussed during each session. The therapist's role is nondirective during the therapy process.

Techniques used in client-centered therapy include:

| | |
|---|---|
| **Unconditional positive regard** | The client is accepted totally by the therapist. The therapist always portrays a positive, nonjudgmental attitude toward the client. |
| **Empathy** | The therapist attempts to see the world through the client's eyes in order to achieve an accurate understanding of the client's emotions. |
| **Congruence** | Also known as **genuineness** or **realness**. Therapist does not maintain a formal attitude, but rather expresses what she/he genuinely feels – strives to be **authentic**. |
| **Reflection** | Technique whereby the therapist serves as a psychological "mirror" by communicating back to the client a summary of what |

was said or what emotion the client seems to be expressing.

**Active listening**     Technique in which therapist attempts to understand both the content and emotion of a client's statements.

## Problem Solving Examples:

 What is Rogers' fundamental theory of psychotherapy?

 Rogers contends that people who enter psychotherapy have an incongruence between their conscious self-image and their real self. This causes them to feel anxious and to act defensively. The goal of psychotherapy is to have the client freely explore his thoughts and to establish a realistic self-image that is congruent with his real self, the self that is disguised by a set of parentally or socially imposed values that have no necessary relations to the client's needs. Since the client, in his normal environment, cannot explore his thoughts freely without criticism from others it is necessary to enter into a therapeutic environment.

The Rogerian therapist has the responsibility of viewing the client with unconditional positive regard and to be genuine in his acceptance of the client regardless of what the client says or does. The therapeutic environment must be as unthreatening as possible. The client must feel free to explore his inner self without fear of judgment. It is expected that this unthreatening environment will allow the client to actually experience the feelings that were denied to awareness because they were threatening to the structure of the self-image. The client will find his behavior changing in a constructive fashion as a result of this new freedom.

Rogerian therapy is often referred to as "humanistic" because the outlook of the Rogerian therapist is optimistic. He has faith in the positive side of human nature and believes that there is a potential for every human being to lead a happy life. The therapist's view is extremely distant from the client's view of life. This is true because the client is at a low point in his emotional life and he must draw strength from the therapist to explore his mind and establish his own values. The therapist is supposed to inspire confidence. At the same time, the therapist should not advise or suggest solutions – this would be counter to the theory of Rogerian therapy. This is why the therapy is often called nondirective, the therapist does not direct the client in any way. Because therapy is client-centered, the client is at the center of the process; he does the thinking, talking and solving. The therapist provides the environment in which the client can work. Rogers prefers to refer to the people in therapy as "clients" rather than "patients" because of all the negative connotations of the word "patient."

The results of successful psychotherapy for the client would be openness to experience, absence of defensiveness, accurate awareness, unconditional self-regard, and harmonious relations with others.

 What is the major task of a Rogerian (or client-oriented) therapist?

 The major task of a client-centered therapist is to establish an atmosphere that lets the client be open to experience. By taking the emphasis of therapy away from the search for a cure and focusing on placing the client in a self-developmental and growth situation, the client is able to fully realize his own capabilities and positive characteristics.

A client-centered therapist does not use interpretation to the extent that a Freudian psychoanalyst would; he attempts to be less judgmental and evaluative. Client-centered therapy is the strongest supporter of the need for a client-therapist relationship, the reason being that as the relationship develops, the client is less apprehensive about examining his own feelings and behaviors.

 What basic factor distinguishes client-centered therapy from the more classical therapies?

**A** The basic factor that distinguishes client-centered therapy from other therapies is that client-centered therapy does not view human nature as self-destructive, defensive, or irrational.

Client-centered therapy, developed by Carl Rogers, views man as the possessor of an innate capacity and motivation towards positive self-fulfillment or actualization. Consistent with this optimistic view of human nature is Rogers' belief that all behavior is selected with the self-fulfillment goal in mind and that although some behavior choices might prove to be self-damaging, the intention is always positive in its orientation.

Another important factor in client-centered therapy is the attempt by the therapist to remain as non-directive as possible during therapy sessions. The ultimate goal is for the client to develop his own solutions to problems.

Also unique to Rogers is his emphasis on researching his own techniques to examine their efficacy.

The goal of **Gestalt therapy** is for clients to become aware of what they are doing and how they can change, while learning to accept and value themselves. This therapy is most often associated with **Fritz Perls**. The word Gestalt means **whole** or complete. The Gestalt therapist helps individuals rebuild thinking and feeling into connected wholes. Gestalt therapy is more **directive** than either client-centered therapy or existential therapy.

Working either one-to-one in individual therapy or in a group therapy setting, the Gestalt therapist encourages individuals to become more aware of their immediate experience. The emphasis is on what is happening here and now rather than what happened in the past or what may happen in the future. It focuses on what really exists rather than on what is absent and on what is real rather than on what is fantasy. The therapist also helps promote awareness by drawing attention to the client's voice, posture, and movements. Gestalt therapists often confront and challenge clients with evidence of their defensiveness, game playing, etc.

## Problem Solving Example:

 Describe Gestalt therapy and what principles are used in treating neurosis.

Conceived by Fritz Perls, Gestalt psychology, as its name implies, aims at helping a patient become a whole, integrated person. This theory is comprised of a mixture of psychoanalytic and existential concepts. Its main premise is that neurotic behavior or personality disorders are a result of a lack of integration of various aspects within an individual. The painful or undesirable aspects of a disturbed person's personality have not been accepted by him; this leaves him fragmented, confused, and ineffective. The aim of therapy is to bring the self-awareness of the individual to include the presently unacceptable parts. This assimilation process begins to make the person more of a "whole person," which translated into behavior means a more effective, self-reliant, authentic, loving person.

The therapy often takes place within a group, but the focus is on the individual. Individuals work through their problem in front of the group when they are ready to do so. Though past experience is seen as important and instrumental in determining a person's particular problem, the solution to these problems is thought to be in the present. Focus within therapy is on the "now" – the experience of the individual during the present moment.

Dream and fantasy interpretations are used by Gestalt therapists. They consider that every object of the dream or fantasy is a part of the person. Patients are encouraged, during role playing sessions, to act out the parts of the people and inanimate objects in their dreams and fantasies. For instance, if one has a dream about crossing a bridge in a small car with a friend, one would be asked to play the part of the bridge, the small car, and the friend.

All communication between the therapist and the group is to be in the present tense. NOW is the most important concept in Gestalt therapy. The use of the word "I" is also encouraged so that people will begin to assume more personal responsibility for their behavior. The tendency of neurotic patients to avoid unpleasant feelings that occur is confronted by asking that group members hold onto the unpleasant emotional experiences. They are then asked to elaborate on the experience in order to work it out and understand it more fully as part of a self that has been denied or ignored.

**Existential therapy** is a humanistic approach to therapy that addresses the meaning of life and allows clients to devise a system of values that gives purpose to their lives. It is based on the premise that the inability to deal with freedom can produce anguish, fear, and concern. The goal of therapy is for clients to come to grips with the freedoms they have, to understand how they fit in with the rest of the world, and to give them more meaning for their lives. The importance of free choice or free will is emphasized.

The existential therapist may be directive in therapy to probe and challenge clients' views of the world. **Confrontation** may be used whereby clients are challenged to examine the quality of their existence. When successful, existential therapy often brings about a reappraisal of what is important in life.

## Problem Solving Example:

Explain the concepts of existential neurosis and logotherapy.

Victor Frankl, a survivor of the German concentration camps of World War II, has focused his theoretical writings and his therapy procedures on his patients' frequent complaints that their lives lack meaning or purpose. This experience of the futile, empty meaninglessness of life – a contemporary disorder – is sometimes called an existential neurosis, characterized by an alienation from society and self. Its key components are the pervasive sense of meaninglessness, loneliness, boredom, apathy, and lack of direction. Frankl called this collection of symptoms the "existential vacuum" which he attributed in part to the decline of historical traditions and values, including religion. He believes that this decline in values has left people with an inner vacuum that has prevented them from identifying values and a direction in life.

The individual suffering from this modern neurosis lacks a sense of personal identity and has a tendency to view himself as an automaton, good for nothing more than assuming a social role which some other automaton could just as easily do. These people may even be quite good at performing their roles in life, but they do so without real commitment, involvement, or purpose. The more obvious symptoms of the existential neurosis are often precipitated when some obstacle or stress within the environment interferes with the enactment of the roles they usually play and reveals their inadequacies.

The treatment that Frankl has devised to treat this disturbance is called "logotherapy." The purpose of the therapy is to help the patient find a purpose for living, a meaning to life. From his experience and work, Frankl decided that this "will to meaning" was the prime motivator of human beings, and that the "will to pleasure," the "will to power" or "self-actualization drives" were all secondary and of service to the will to meaning. He believes that man is constantly reaching out for a meaning to fulfill and that by virtue of his ability to transcend himself, he is always seeking to serve a cause higher than himself or to lose his self-preoccupation by loving another person.

### 6.2.4 Cognitive Therapies

**Cognitive therapies** are insight therapies that emphasize recognizing and changing negative thoughts and maladaptive beliefs. Cognitive therapists argue that people have psychological disorders because their thinking is inappropriate or maladaptive. The goal of therapy is to change or restructure clients' thinking.

**Cognitive-behavior therapy** is a blending of behavioral therapy (described in section 6.3) and cognitive therapy.

Albert Ellis and Aaron Beck are the two best known cognitive therapists.

**Rational-Emotive Therapy (RET)** was developed by **Albert Ellis**. RET encourages people to examine their beliefs carefully and rationally, to make positive statements about themselves, and to solve problems effectively.

Rational-emotive therapy is based on Ellis' **ABC theory**. **A** refers to the **activating** event, **B** to the person's **belief** about the event, and **C** to the emotional **consequence** that follows. Ellis claimed that **A** does not cause **C**, but instead **B** causes **C**. If the **belief** is irrational, then the emotional consequence can be extreme distress.

Ellis felt that many beliefs are irrational. For instance, many people hold irrational **should beliefs** (e.g., "I **should** be perfect!"). Because it is impossible to live up to these irrational "should" beliefs, people are doomed to frustration and unhappiness.

Rational-emotive therapy is a **directive, confrontational** form of therapy that is designed to challenge clients' irrational beliefs about themselves and others. It helps clients replace irrational beliefs with rational ones that are appropriate and less distressing. Rational-emotive therapists do not believe that a warm relationship between therapist and client is necessary for the therapy to be effective.

Another cognitive therapy that focuses on irrational beliefs is that of **Aaron Beck**. Beck's theory assumes that depression and anxiety are caused by people's distorted views of reality. These distorted views cause clients to have negative views of the world, others, and themselves. Beck felt that many depressed and anxious people have **automatic thoughts** or unreasonable ideas that rule their lives.

The goal of therapy, according to Beck, is to help clients stop their negative thoughts and to help them develop realistic thinking about the situations they encounter. The therapist challenges clients' irrational thoughts, and clients are often given homework assignments, such as keeping track of automatic thoughts and then substituting more rational thoughts.

### 6.2.5 Evaluating Insight Therapies

It is difficult to evaluate the effectiveness of any psychotherapy. For instance, **spontaneous remission** sometimes occurs when psychological disorders clear up on their own without treatment or therapy. Because of the possibility of spontaneous remission, if clients seem to "get better" after therapy, you cannot automatically assume that this recovery was due to the treatment.

Judging the effectiveness of insight therapies is especially difficult because it is often unclear what to measure and who to ask. For instance, do you ask the client or the therapist? Do you measure behavior or emotions?

Results from **meta-analysis**, a mathematical technique that summarizes the outcomes of many different studies, indicate that insight therapy results in a better outcome than no treatment about 75 to 80% of the time. Only a few clients (around 10%) are worse off after therapy.

Individuals who seem to have the best response to insight therapies are intelligent, successful people. These are individuals who are also highly motivated and who have positive attitudes about therapy. Clients who are less severely disturbed are more likely to benefit than those with more severe pathology.

## 6.3 Behavioral Therapies

**Behavioral therapies** are based on the assumption that both normal and abnormal behaviors are learned. Treatment consists, therefore, of either learning a new "normal" behavior or unlearning a maladaptive behavior. Behavior therapies are built upon classical and operant conditioning as well as imitation and social learning. Behavioral therapies are often referred to as **behavior modification**.

### 6.3.1 Types of Therapies

Several therapies based on classical conditioning, operant or instrumental conditioning, and social learning have been developed.

**Classical conditioning** occurs whenever a neutral stimulus acquires the ability to evoke a response that was originally triggered by another stimulus. Systematic desensitization and aversion therapy are two therapies based on the classical conditioning approach.

**Systematic desensitization** is a behavior therapy used to reduce clients' anxiety and fear responses through counterconditioning. **Counterconditioning** is a process of reconditioning in which a person is taught a new, more adaptive response to a stimulus. For instance, instead of displaying a fear response when confronted with a frightening situation, clients are counterconditioned to display a relaxed response.

Systematic desensitization is a three-step process:

**Step 1**   The therapist and client construct a **hierarchy of fears**. The client ranks (from the least amount to the greatest amount of fear) specific situations that arouse anxiety.

**Step 2**   The client is trained in relaxation techniques.

**Step 3**   The client works through the hierarchy of fears while practicing the relaxation techniques learned in Step 2.

Systematic desensitization is based on the premise that anxiety and relaxation are incompatible responses. It has proven very effective in dealing with fears, phobias, and anxiety.

**Flooding** is another behavioral technique used to help clients overcome fears, and it is almost the opposite of systematic desensitization. During flooding, clients are exposed to the fear all at once for an extended period until their anxiety decreases. Flooding can be successful because it shows clients that none of the dreaded consequences they expect actually happen.

**Aversion therapy** is another therapy based on classical conditioning. It is also a form of counterconditioning that pairs an aversive or noxious stimulus with a stimulus that elicits an undesired behavior. For instance, aversion therapy has been used to treat alcoholics. The therapist might administer a drug that causes nausea and vomiting whenever alcohol is consumed. By pairing the drug with alcohol, the therapist hopes to create a conditioned aversion to alcohol.

**Operant** or **instrumental conditioning** occurs whenever voluntary responses come to be controlled by their consequences. Token economies, contingency contracting, time-out, extinction, and punishment are therapeutic approaches based on operant conditioning.

| | |
|---|---|
| **Token economies** | Desired behaviors are rewarded with tokens that can later be exchanged for desired objects or privileges. Clients are "fined" (i.e., must return some tokens) for inappropriate behaviors. Often used in institutional settings, such as schools, hospitals, etc. |
| **Contingency contracting** | A written agreement is drawn up between the therapist and client that states behavioral objectives the client hopes to attain. Contracts usually state positive consequences or rewards for meeting the objectives and sometimes include negative consequences if goals are not met. |
| **Time-out** | Used to eliminate undesirable behavior, usually with children. It involves moving the individual away from all reinforcement for a period of time. |
| **Extinction** | Occurs when a maladaptive behavior is not followed by reinforcers. Often involves ignoring a behavior. |
| **Punishment** | Occurs when behavior is followed by an aversive stimulus. The goal is to eliminate the inappropriate behavior and is often combined with positive reinforcement for appropriate behavior. |

**Observational Learning and Modeling** occurs when children and adults learn behaviors by observing others. According to **Albert Bandura**, modeling is most effective for learning new behavior by helping to eliminate fears (by watching others engage in the feared behavior or interact with the feared object) and encouraging the expression of already existing behavior.

People can also learn inappropriate or maladaptive behaviors by observing others.

**Participant modeling** is a technique that occurs when the model not only demonstrates the appropriate behavior in graduated steps, but the client attempts to imitate the model step by step. The therapist provides encouragement and support.

**Social skills training** is a behavioral therapy designed to improve interpersonal skills and emphasizes modeling, behavioral rehearsal, and shaping.

### 6.3.2 Evaluating Behavioral Therapies

Behavioral therapies appear to be the most successful with certain kinds of problems. For instance, they have been reported to work well for phobias, compulsive behaviors, controlling impulses, and learning new social skills to replace maladaptive ones.

Behavioral therapies have been criticized because they emphasize external behavior and ignore internal thoughts and expectations. Behavioral therapies have also been criticized for focusing on the symptom, without searching for what it might symbolize. Additionally, they are not well suited to treat some types of problems.

## Problem Solving Examples:

 Describe the different techniques used in behavior therapy.

 Behavior therapy, also called behavior modification, is an attempt to study and change abnormal behavior by drawing on the methods used by experimental psychologists in their study of normal behavior. Four different techniques of behavior therapy can be distinguished:

1) counterconditioning,

2) operant conditioning,

3) modeling, and

4) cognitive restructuring.

In counterconditioning, an undesired response to a given stimulus is eliminated by calling forth a new response in the presence of that stimulus. Suppose that a child has nyctophobia – fear of the dark. Whenever he finds himself in a dark place (stimulus), he experiences intense feelings of anxiety (undesired response). The goal of counterconditioning would be to elicit a new, positive response in the young client while he is confronted with darkness. This might be achieved by feeding the child one of his favorite foods in the dark. In this fashion, the fear (undesired response) produced by darkness (stimulus) might be dispelled by the positive feelings (new response) associated with eating. Repeated associations of darkness with positive feelings would most likely cure the client of his phobia.

Three frequently used counterconditioning techniques are:

a) systematic desensitization,

b) assertive training, and

c) aversive conditioning.

Systematic desensitization, formulated by Joseph Wolpe, is a procedure in which a deeply relaxed person is asked to imagine a series of anxiety-provoking situations, along a continuum. For example, a person who is afraid of taking tests will first be told to imagine the teacher telling the class of an upcoming test; then he'll be told to think of himself studying for the test and finally, he must imagine he is actually taking the test. This procedure may require more intermediary steps, in which the person is told to imagine more scenes before the final one, which is more anxiety producing. The number of additional steps depends on the level of anxiety. The relaxation serves to inhibit any anxiety that might otherwise be produced by the imagined scenes. The imagined scene can be viewed as the stimulus; the anxiety elicited by the scene is the undesired response, and relaxation is the new response. It has been found that the ability to tolerate stressful imagery is generally followed by a reduction of anxiety in similar real-life situations.

Assertive training is helpful to those people who are unable to express positive or negative feelings to others. For example, consider a man who is often treated rudely by a business associate but is too timid to protest or express resentment. Because of his suppressed negative feelings, he experiences anxiety whenever he comes into contact with the business associate. Assertive training assumes that expression of positive or negative feelings can countercondition the anxiety associated with specific interpersonal situations. Applying this assumption to our example, the anxiety (undesired response) elicited by the presence of the rude business associate (stimulus) would be counteracted if the timid man were to express his true feelings to the associate (new response).

Another variant of counterconditioning is aversive conditioning, which attempts to attach negative feelings to stimuli that are considered inappropriately attractive. Imagine that a foot fetishist wishes to be less attracted to the sight or feel of feet. To reduce the attraction, a therapist might give him repeated electric shocks as pictures of feet are presented. The goal of such therapy would be to make feet (stimulus) elicit anxiety (new response) rather than feelings of attraction (undesired response).

Operant conditioning, also known as behavior shaping, is another technique of behavior therapy. The principles of operant conditioning are very straightforward: behaviors whose frequency it is desirable to increase are rewarded and behaviors whose frequency it is desirable to decrease are either ignored or punished. Operant conditioning has been applied to the populations of many mental institutions in the form of a token economy. Patients are systematically reinforced with plastic tokens that can later be exchanged for goods and privileges. The results of such programs have been very encouraging. Operant conditioning has also been successful in the treatment of children with behavior problems.

A third technique of behavior therapy is modeling, which involves learning by observing and imitating the behavior of others. As an example, examine how modeling would be used to rid a client of a dog phobia. The therapist might expose the client to both live and filmed displays of people interacting fearlessly with dogs. Hopefully, the client would imitate the models he has been exposed to and eventually overcome his fear of dogs. A number of research programs have shown that this kind of learning is helping people acquire new responses in a relatively short time.

Cognitive restructuring, the fourth technique of behavior modification, attempts to directly manipulate the thinking and reasoning processes of the client. Perhaps the best example of a cognitive restructuring procedure is rational-emotive therapy, which has developed from the work of Albert Ellis. Rational-emotive therapy assumes:

1) people cognitively interpret what is happening around them;

2) sometimes these interpretations can cause emotional turmoil; and

3) a therapist's attention should be focused on these internal sentences and not on historical causes. An example of an internal belief which may lead to distress is the notion that it is imperative to be thoroughly competent in everything one does. A person functioning with this idea in mind will view every error he makes as a catastrophe. A rational-emotive therapist would help such a client by first making him aware of the irrational structure under which he is living and then guiding him towards a belief in realistic goals.

 How is aversion therapy used in treating a patient with a particular fetish?

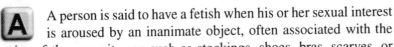 A person is said to have a fetish when his or her sexual interest is aroused by an inanimate object, often associated with the attire of the opposite sex such as stockings, shoes, bras, scarves, or

hats. Some merely collect these items and use them in their sexual imaginings and masturbation activities; others need to have these objects present to have a successful sexual encounter with another person. Without the fetish object, the person may be incapable of normal sexual response.

Learning theory explains that the fetish object is accidentally associated with earlier gratifying sexual experiences. The object may have been within the environment during his or her first pleasurable sexual encounter. Each repetition of a successful sexual experience with the object reinforces the connection between the object and gratification and thereby makes it a more effective and attractive stimulus.

To undo this learning process, a behavior therapist might use behavior modification technique of aversive therapy. The procedure used in aversive therapy is the pairing of a stimulus with negative reinforcement so that the patient eventually comes to develop negative associations with the stimulus. For instance, a movie screen might be used to show varieties of the fetish object, and the patient, while watching the movie, would receive mild electric shock each time a new image of the arousing object was presented.

This technique has proven to be relatively successful in treating fetishism. However, fetishism is typically associated with a wide range of unusual sexual behaviors which would each have to be treated separately using behavior modification techniques. It is becoming clearer that a combined approach of analytic and behavior modification techniques is the most effective treatment for a variety of behavior disorders including fetishism. Uncovering both the childhood experiences that may have established the fetish and other unusual sexual behaviors would provide the patient with insight about his problem. Once the patient has acquired this understanding, learning techniques, such as aversive therapy, can be more likely to result in a long-term, pervasive change in behavior.

## 6.4 Biological Treatments

The **biological perspective** views abnormal behavior as a symptom of an underlying physical disorder and usually favors biological therapy.

### 6.4.1 Drug Treatments

**Psychopharmacotherapy** is the treatment of mental disorders with medication. This is often referred to as **drug therapy**. Drugs used to treat mental disorders are categorized based on their effects and are described below.

**Antipsychotics (Neuropleptics)**

Gradually reduce psychotic symptoms, such as hallucinations, delusions, paranoia, disordered thinking, and incoherence. Between 60 and 70% show improvement when taking these drugs.

*Side-effects* include drowsiness, constipation, dry mouth, muscular rigidity, and impaired coordination. Can cause **tardive dyskinesia** or permanent chronic tremors and involuntary muscle movements.

*Examples*: Haldol, Mellaril, Thorazine, and Clozapine.

**Antidepressants**

Designed to relieve symptoms of depression. About 60 – 70% of patients who take these drugs report an improved mood. Depressive symptoms are not affected until two to six weeks after drug therapy begins.

*Side-effects* can include sleepiness and may be dangerous if mixed with alcohol.

*Examples*: Tofranil, Elavil, Prozac, Anafranil, and Nardil.

**Antianxiety Drugs (Anxiolytics)**

Commonly called **tranquilizers**, these mood – altering substances are calming, reduce anxiety and stress, and lower excitability. They are the most widely prescribed of all legal drugs.

*Side-effects:* Some can cause physical dependence and withdrawal symptoms if abruptly discontinued.

*Examples:* Librium, Valium, Xanax, BuSpar, Equanil, Miltown, and Tranxene.

**Antimania Drug (Lithium)**

If taken regularly, **lithium carbonate** is about 80% effective in preventing both the depression and mania associated with bipolar disorder. Dosage must be exact and constantly monitored, however, because too little has no effect and too much can be deadly. It takes a week or two of regular use before results are evident.

*Side-effects*: Vomiting, nausea, tremor, fatigue, slurred speech; overdose can result in death.

*Examples:* Lithium carbonate and Eskalith.

## Problem Solving Examples:

When was the advent of pharmacological therapy in the U.S.?

The advent of pharmacological therapy began with the introduction of a drug called chlorpromazine in 1952. Chlorpromazine, also known as Thorazine, is a synthetic drug. It was initially used to control violent symptoms in psychotics.

Before the introduction of drugs into therapy, physical restraint was the most common form of patient control. Aside from some barbiturate usage, many patients were also controlled with pre-frontal lobotomies, electro-convulsive shocks, and insulin-shock therapy. The introduction of pharmacological agents into daily use at mental hospitals revolutionized the field of clinical psychology.

 Describe the development and use of common psychotogenic drugs in use today.

Psychotogenic drugs cause the production of unusual and exaggerated mental effects. Also known as hallucinogens and psychedelics, these drugs mostly affect the perceptual and cognitive functioning of the individual. The most common examples of psychotogenic drugs are lysergic acid diethylamide (LSD), psilocybin, and mescaline.

LSD is the most widely referred to and most dangerous psychotogenic drug in use today. It is an extremely potent drug (4,000 times stronger than mescaline) and has been used in a variety of ways since its discovery in 1943. Its ingestion is accompanied by hallucinations and perceptual distortions; research indicates an impairment of simple cognitive functions as well.

In the area of psychological research, LSD was once considered a key to schizophrenia (since it exhibits a "model" psychosis) and an aid in psychotherapeutic techniques. Both of these contentions have not been substantiated by research and were subsequently rejected. LSD has been useful in the study of the neurochemical functioning of the brain because of its similarity to serotonin.

## 6.4.2  Electroconvulsive Therapy (ECT)

In 1938 Italian physicians **Ugo Cerletti** and **Lucio Bini** created seizures in patients by passing an electric current through their brains. During the 1940s and 1950s **electroconvulsive therapy (ECT)** or **shock treatment** was routinely used to treat depression, schizophrenia, and sometimes mania. It was often used on patients who did not need it. Today ECT is an uncommon treatment and is used mainly as a last resort treatment for severe depression. No one knows for sure how or why ECT works. The seizure that results from ECT may temporarily change the biochemical balance in the brain, which results in a decrease of depressive symptoms. The effects of ECT are only temporary if not followed by drug therapy and psychotherapy. Up to 100,000 people receive ECT each year.

Typically, patients are anesthetized and given a muscle relaxant. ECT occurs by placing two electrodes on a patient's head and sending a mild electric current through the brain for one or two seconds. Immediately after the shock, the patient loses consciousness and experiences a seizure that lasts up to one minute. The entire ECT procedure takes about five minutes and the risk of death or any medical complication is very rare. However, there is a potential for memory loss and a decreased ability to learn and retain new information for up to several weeks following the procedure.

## Problem Solving Example:

 How effective is electroconvulsive shock therapy in schizophrenia, in depression?

In the 1930s it was believed that a biological antagonism existed between schizophrenia and convulsions. Therefore, it was determined that the inducement of convulsions in schizophrenic patients might be therapeutic. For some years the drug metrazol was used to induce convulsions in patients. The drug had the disadvantage of causing extreme fear in patients and of being unpredictable about the degree of seizure it caused. In the 1940s, the use of electroconvulsive shock treatment (ECT) came to be widely used because it caused immediate unconsciousness in the patient. Thus, there was no time for a fear reaction and the doses could be controlled so that extreme convulsions could be avoided.

ECT involves the passage of a 100-volt electric current across electrodes placed at the patient's temples. The current causes immediate unconsciousness and is followed by what appears to be a mild epileptic seizure. Today, prior to administering the shock, the patient is usually given a muscle relaxant to reduce the severity of the convulsions during the seizure. ECT drastically reduces the amount of oxygen in the brain due to the high level of brain activity that occurs during the electroshock which depletes the supply of oxygen and glucose.

It has been shown that, contrary to the 1930s hypothesis that convulsions are an effective treatment for schizophrenia; these treatments are essentially ineffective for schizophrenic patients. However, they have been used in the treatment of depressive patients who can not be treated successfully with medication. The usual procedure consists of 10 to 14 treatments spread over several weeks. The after-effects of the treatments include temporary loss of memory, disorientation and confusion. These effects usually disappear within a month or two after the treatments, but are one of the reasons why this type of therapy is resisted by patients.

Today ECT is used sometimes as a last resort for severely depressed patients. No valid scientific explanation for the usefulness of ECT has been thus far offered. One theory is that the temporary improvement noted after shock treatment may be due to the mobilization of resources to a real threat to existence. A social learning theory suggests that the punishment character of the shock serves as negative reinforcement for the depressive behavior.

### 6.4.3 Psychosurgery

**Psychosurgery** is brain surgery and is an even more drastic procedure than ECT described above. Psychosurgery has been performed in the past to relieve the symptoms of serious psychological disorders, such as severe depression, severe obsessions or anxiety, and, in some cases, of unbearable chronic pain. It is not the same as brain surgery that is performed to correct a physical problem.

In 1937, **Egas Moniz** introduced a surgical technique called **prefrontal lobotomy**. In the 1940s and 1950s prefrontal lobotomies were routinely performed during which the frontal lobes of the brain were surgically separated from the deeper brain centers involved in emotion. No brain tissue was removed. Eventually it became apparent that this surgery often left patients in a severely deteriorated condition (i.e., impaired intellect, loss of motivation, personality changes) and was no cure-all for mental illness.

The advent of antipsychotic drugs in the mid-1950s ended most psychosurgery. Today, psychosurgery is performed only in rare cases where all else has failed and involves the destruction of only a tiny amount of brain tissue.

## Problem Solving Example:

**Q** What are the potential benefits and difficulties with psycho-surgery and what other type of therapy is often substituted for psychosurgery?

**A** Psychosurgery, a most drastic form of physical therapy that is generally not used today, was pioneered in the 1930s by Moniz and Freeman. This treatment consists of various surgical procedures including the slicing, puncturing, or removal of certain areas of the prefrontal lobes of the brain. The theory underlying this approach was that severing the nerve connections with the thalamus, which was then believed to be the controlling center for the emotions, would relieve severe emotional disturbance.

In certain cases, this procedure turned unmanageable patients into more docile creatures. But in the majority of cases, patients were left with irreversible brain damage. Many were turned into listless, lifeless, insensitive human beings. Thus, psychosurgery has been restricted for use with a limited number of patients. It has been found to be effective in reducing the extreme pain associated with certain forms of terminal cancer.

Other physical therapy treatments for mental patients that are gaining popularity today include electroconvulsive shock therapy and drug therapy. Antidepressant, anti-manic, antipsychotic and antianxiety drugs are all in great use today. Since the early 1950s, when psychopharmaceutical drugs were discovered, the care of mental patients has been revolutionized. Though drugs have not been shown to have a curative effect, they are highly effective in dealing with the symptoms associated with a wide range of disorders during their natural course.

## 6.5   Community Mental Health

**Community psychology** is a movement that attempts to minimize or prevent mental disorders, not just treat them. Rather than emphasizing hospitalization or one-on-one therapy sessions, the community psychology approach focuses on the **prevention** of psychological disorders.

During the 1960s, the mental health system adopted a program of **deinstitutionalization**, discharging people from mental hospitals into the community, hopefully into a supportive environment of family and friends. The efforts to integrate the chronically mentally ill into the community have, for the most part, failed.

The community mental health approach argues that effective treatment for mental illness requires a variety of different organizations and services. These include **crisis hotlines, family consultation** and **family therapy, halfway houses, long-term outpatient care**, some **short-term inpatient care, job training, day care**, and other supportive services.

# CHAPTER 7

# Social Behavior

## 7.1 Attitudes and Attitude Change

**Social psychology** is the branch of psychology concerned with the way individuals' thoughts, feelings, and behaviors are influenced by others.

**Social cognition** involves the mental processes associated with how people perceive and react to others.

**Attitudes** are beliefs and opinions that can predispose individuals to behave in certain ways.

Social psychologists have defined **three components** of attitudes:

**Cognitive Component**      Includes the beliefs and ideas held about the object of an attitude.

**Affective Component**      The emotional feelings stimulated by an attitude.

**Behavioral Component**      The predispositions to act in certain ways that are relevant to one's attitude.

The relationship between attitudes and behavior is complicated. You cannot predict specific behavior by knowing someone's attitude. **Situational demands** and **constraints** may lead to inconsistent relationships between attitudes and behavior.

The **mere exposure effect** predicts that our attitude toward something or someone will become more positive with continued exposure.

# Problem Solving Examples:

 What is social psychology? What features differentiate it from other behavioral sciences?

In the study of human behavior, social psychology focuses particularly on the psychology of the individual in society. More particularly, it investigates the influence process of that society as it acts on the individual. To this end, social psychologists may draw from sociology and cultural anthropology, but their primary interest is still the psychological level. This discipline is not, as many assume, a combination of sociological and psychological concepts; rather it is a field that has generated its own unique approach to the analysis of social processes, based on concepts from the level of individual psychology to that of wider social behavior.

Social behavior is the main thrust of social psychological research. Through the use of the scientific method and objective study, a body of knowledge has been produced that is helping us to understand the underlying processes in social interactions. Again, the most distinctive feature of social psychology is its emphasis on individual psychology in terms of individual perceptions, motivations, and learning to account for the interaction of the individual and the society of which the individual is a part.

Within the field of social psychology, there are wide ranges of thought and explanations of social behavior which run from the psychoanalytic to the behavioristic. However, there are two main theoretical schools of thought that can be readily differentiated. The theorists that concentrate more on the internal processes of the individual and his cognitive processes are called the cognitive theorists. They believe the human being is an organizer and processor of experience; that his "world view" contributes greatly to his social behavior. More emphasis is placed on external events by the behaviorists, who tend to adhere to the belief that people are reactors to the events that occur around them. These scientists tend to focus, therefore, on the world external to the individual in explaining his behavior.

The experimental method is the research method used by most all social psychologists, regardless of their theoretical position. At the core of all experiments is the following basic question: do changes in one variable (the "independent variable") produce changes in another variable (the "dependent variable")? In this way the body of knowledge coming out of social psychology rests firmly on the scientific method. A question that the student might, however, wish to ask is, "can the scientific method adequately measure all aspects of human psychology?" This is a large question, not to be addressed in this brief space, but one which must be asked by the serious student of human behavior.

 Give a brief history of the study of social behavior.

Social psychology, as we know it, is a modern discipline, but the behavior of an individual human being as part of the larger society has been of interest to man since antiquity. In tracing the history of this interest, there can be seen three distinct periods in the development of social psychology as it exists today: the philosophical, statistical, and analytical periods.

The philosophical approach to individual behavior in social groupings can be found as far back as 2000 B.C. in the Babylonian Code of Hammurabi. We are more familiar with the more recent thoughts of Aristotle and Plato on the role of man in society. The philosophical approach relied mainly on the power of thought apart from testable data; that is, it relied more on reason or the authority of the writer than on any systematic gathering of factual information. Many of the great thinkers on human nature are part of the "roots" of social psychological thought: Hobbes, Rousseau, Kant, Diderot, Goethe, Freud, and Darwin have all contributed to our conceptions of the interaction of society and the individual human being. This philosophical tradition and approach, as we can see, dominates the history of social psychology for the next stage, the statistical or empirical stage, only began approximately 100 years ago with the work of Francis Galton on human genetics.

During this stage in the development of social psychology emphasis was on the description of human traits and the conditions of human society. Generally, it relies upon systematic data gathering to obtain information about the conditions of human nature and life. Galton, inspired by Charles Darwin's views on natural selection, conducted research on the transmission of genius genetically by tracing the history of families whose members had attained great prominence. Also in this tradition is the work of Binet in standardizing tests for human intelligence; Durkheim, who collected statistics on suicide; and the work of the demographists – scientists who study population characteristics. Data gathering had begun.

If the statistical stage began to provide factual descriptive characteristics of human characteristics, then the analytical period, which began at about the turn of the last century, is the move toward probing beneath the descriptive data to understand the causal factors in that data. This is the stage in which we find social psychology today. It is now concerned with establishing scientifically valid foundations for what it observes.

### 7.1.1 Cognitive Dissonance

**Cognitive dissonance** is the conflict that arises when a person holds two or more attitudes that are inconsistent. Cognitive dissonance theory was developed by social psychologist **Leon Festinger**. When in a state of cognitive dissonance, Festinger suggested we feel uneasy and are thereby motivated to make our attitudes consistent.

An example of dissonant cognitions would be, "I smoke, yet I believe that smoking is unhealthy." Festinger's theory predicts that these two thoughts would lead to a state of cognitive dissonance. Efforts to reduce this dissonance will probably cause attitudes to change. This could reduce dissonance by one of the following:

Modifying one or both of the cognitions.

*Example*: "I really don't smoke that much."

Changing the perceived importance of one of the cognitions.

*Example*: "Most of the research is done with laboratory rats and rats seem to get cancer from everything."

Adding cognitions.

*Example*: "I exercise more than the average person and eat healthy foods."

Denying the two cognitions are related to each other.

*Example*: "I don't know any smokers who have died from lung cancer."

**Festinger** and **Carlsmith** in 1959 demonstrated cognitive dissonance in a classic experiment. In one condition, subjects were offered $1 to describe a dull, boring task as interesting. A control group was offered $20 to describe the task as interesting. Festinger and Carlsmith reasoned that subjects paid $20 to tell a lie would not experience dissonance because they had a good reason or justification for their behavior – $20. Subjects paid $1, however, should experience cognitive dissonance because they told a lie for little justification. Just as they predicted, subjects paid $1 actually rated the task as more enjoyable, thereby reducing their dissonance, than subjects who were paid $20.

**Effort justification** is another example of cognitive dissonance. We tend to rate more favorably those experiences, items, etc. that require more effort to obtain. **Aronson** and **Mills** in 1959 demonstrated effort justification by finding that college students who went through a more severe initiation in order to join what turned out to be a boring group, later rated the group as more enjoyable than did a group that did not go through any initiation.

**Selective exposure** occurs when we attempt to minimize dissonance by exposing ourselves only to information that supports a choice we have made.

An alternative theoretical explanation for cognitive dissonance was suggested by **Darryl Bem**. Bem's **self-perception** theory states that people form attitudes by observing their own behavior and by applying the same principles to themselves as they do to others. That is, when we are unclear about the reasons we have engaged in a certain behavior, we look at our behavior and try to figure out why we did what we did. For instance, if I agreed to say a boring task was interesting for only a dollar, the task must have been interesting or else I wouldn't have done it.

## Problem Solving Examples:

What is the role of psychological inconsistency in the theory of cognitive dissonance?

Proposed by Leon Festinger, the theory of cognitive dissonance states that people are motivated to keep their cognitions – beliefs, attitudes, opinions, and values – consistent. If the relationship between their cognitions becomes inconsistent, it causes psychological distress which is called "dissonance." Since this state is quite unpleasant to most people, it produces a motivation to change either the attitude or action that is responsible for the dissonance. The more important the attitudes and behavior involved in the dissonance-producing situation, the stronger will be the motivation to change the situation to produce consistency. For example, if a person believes there is a relationship between smoking and cancer and continues to smoke heavily, there is a likelihood that he will experience psychological discomfort upon realizing the inconsistency between the attitude that smoking is dangerous to health and life and the action of smoking.

A key idea is that a person must realize that there is inconsistency before a true state of psychological inconsistency is produced. Often when there is inconsistency in beliefs and actions, people rationalize their behavior. The smoker might also hold the attitude that he was the exception – that while it might be true that the health of many people is endangered by heavy smoking, his health would not be. An individual would personally have to experience the inconsistency in his or her cognitions in order to be motivated to change either attitudes or behavior.

When individuals experience dissonance, they also actively avoid situations that produce this dissonance. Festinger conducted a study on smoking habits and attitudes and discovered that 29 percent of non-smokers, 20 percent of light smokers, but only 7 percent of heavy smokers thought that a relationship existed between smoking and lung cancer. To continue smoking with the strong belief that it would cause danger to one's health causes dissonance, and as we see from this study is not common. (This study was done in 1957; today, with more information available on the effects of smoking on health, we might expect these figures to be different). Dissonance motivates a person to change, to not remain in the dissonance-producing situation, or to adopt a new attitude to the situation.

 Contrast the learning theorists' explanation of the process of attitude change with that of the consistency theorists.

Learning theorists contend that for attitudes to change, rewards or incentives must be offered. Consistency theorists agree that rewards must be offered but hold that psychological inconsistency or imbalance is an equally important factor in producing attitude change.

Both sets of theorists agree with McGuire that the two most popular and effective ways of producing attitude change are to present the subject with a persuasive message and to get him or her involved actively in the attitude-change process. Most of us experience persuasive messages every day in the form of advertising or simply through the attempts of one of our friends, relations or associates to engage our cooperation or our support in some matter. The presentation of persuasive information, while a necessary step in attitude change, if coupled with active participation from the subject, is likely to have much more dramatic effects.

Involving the subject was first observed in traditional psychotherapy. Both Sigmund Freud and Carl Rogers reported that clients who were actively involved in their therapy improved much more than clients who sat passively while the therapist tried to persuade them to change. Kurt Lewin demonstrated in an experimental effort to get homemakers to serve unappetizing, yet nutritional parts of the cow (kidneys, heart), that those that participated in discussion groups attempting to determine how they could induce other homemakers to change their eating habits later were much more likely to serve these meats to their families than those homemakers who simply passively received information about why they should serve these meats. (32% of the active participants and 3% of the persuasive message group later served these organ-meats to their families).

Both learning theorists and consistency theorists agree that active participation produces attitude change, Where they disagree is in the explanation of how and why this occurs. The learning theorists contend that the greater the reward, the more change of attitude will occur. The dissonance theorists, however, claim that the less the reward, the greater the attitude change.

In the case of the homemakers advocating the use of organ-meats, the learning theorists might structure an experiment wherein the participants would receive monetary incentives for giving what their peers judged as the most persuasive talk on why homemakers should consume these parts of the cow. The best speakers might receive $50, $25 and $5 respectively for their efforts. The prediction would be that the persons who received the $50 reward for their presentation would be most likely to serve the meats themselves because the greater incentive motivated these persons to be better advocates for the use of the meats and self-persuasion would be greater and more likely to produce attitude change.

The dissonance theorists would predict that the persons who received no reward would be more likely to use the meat product because the dissonance produced by supporting a subject that one actually was opposed to (most of the women initially objected to the use of these parts of the cow) would not be resolved by the idea that one had done so in order to receive the $50 reward; rather, it would be necessary to change the attitudes to be more in keeping with the behavior of researching and speaking publicly about the great benefits of serving this product. Thus, the smaller the reward, the greater the attitude change.

Which of these diametrically opposed views proves to be correct? Both are correct, but in different situations. The learning theorists' explanation holds true in situations in which the behavior or attitudes involved are seen as relatively unimportant to the person, while the dissonance theorists prove correct when the attitudes involved are viewed as important to the person. Sometimes it is difficult to predict what issues will be important to most people. The case of whether or not the homemakers should serve organ-meats would probably be less important than a debate on group marriage for newlyweds.

### 7.1.2 Persuasion

**Persuasion** occurs when others attempt to change our attitudes. The process of persuasion includes four basic elements: source, receiver, message, and channel.

1.  **The source (or communicator)**

    The source or communicator is the individual who delivers a persuasive message. Communicators are most influential when they have **expertise**, **credibility**, **trustworthiness**, and **power**. **Attractiveness** and **similarity** to the target audience are also important.

2.  **The receiver (target or audience)**

    The receiver, target, or audience is the person to whom a persuasive message is sent. Although the magnitude of differences between women and men is not large, some research suggests that women are more easily persuaded than men. Younger individuals are more likely to change their attitudes than older individuals. If the receiver is not strongly committed to a pre-existing attitude, change is more likely. A **latitude of acceptance** is a range of potentially acceptable positions on an issue, centered on one's initial attitude position. A message that falls within a receiver's latitude of acceptance is much more likely to be persuasive. Information from a persuasive message is processed via a **central route** when the receiver carefully ponders the content and logic of the message. **Peripheral route processing** is taken when persuasion depends on nonmessage factors, such as the attractiveness and credibility of the source and emotional responses. Research suggests that central route processing results in the most lasting attitude change.

3. **Message factors**

   The message is the information transmitted by the source. The less informed we are or the more frightened we are, the more we will be influenced by an emotional message. Positive emotional appeals can be successful, especially through music. **Two-sided arguments** in which both sides of an issue are presented seem to be more effective than one-sided presentations. One-sided messages work when the audience is uneducated about the issue.

4. **The channel or medium**

   The channel is the medium through which the message is sent. Television may be the most powerful medium.

## 7.2  Person Perception

**Person perception** relates to how we form **impressions** of others.

A **person scheme** or **social scheme** is an organized cluster of information, ideas, or impressions about a person. These schemes are not always accurate, however, and can be influenced by physical appearance, first impressions, and stereotypes.

### 7.2.1 Physical Appearance

In general, studies have shown that people have a bias toward viewing attractive men and women as intelligent, competent, talented, pleasant, interesting, kind, and sensitive.

However, people sometimes downplay the talent of successful women who happen to be attractive, attributing their success to their good looks instead of their competence.

### 7.2.2 First Impressions

First impressions can be powerful and can influence many of the later impressions we form about people.

The **primacy effect** is the tendency for early information (i.e., first impressions) to be considered more important than later information about a person when forming impressions. By relying on our first impressions, we do not pay close attention to later information and our first impression becomes a framework through which later impressions are formed.

The primacy effect is helpful in simplifying our impressions if the people we are judging really are consistent.

The primacy effect can lead to person perception errors, however, if the people we are judging are inconsistent in their behavior.

The primacy effect can lead to a **self-fulfilling prophecy** where our expectations influence people to act in ways that confirm our original expectations.

### 7.2.3 Stereotypes, Prejudice, and Discrimination

**Stereotypes** are broad overgeneralizations and widely held beliefs about the way a group of people thinks and acts. The most common stereotypes in our society are based on sex and membership in ethnic and occupational groups. Stereotypes can be positive and negative.

**Prejudice** is a negative attitude toward a group of people that is made without sufficient evidence and is not easily changed. Prejudice includes preconceived hostile and irrational feelings.

**Discrimination** involves action against a person or group of people based on race, ethnicity, class, sex, etc. Discrimination is usually based on prejudice.

Over 40 years ago, **Adorno** and his colleagues wrote that people who are highly prejudiced tend to have **authoritarian personalities** – they tend to be submissive and obedient to authority and to reject other groups in a punitive way. Authoritarian personalities tend to divide people into **in-groups** or **out-groups** and often had harsh and punitive parents. Adorno developed the **California F scale** to measure authoritarianism.

The **scapegoat theory** of stereotypes proposed that people who are frustrated and unhappy about something will choose a relatively powerless group to take the blame for a situation that is not their fault.

The **social identity theory** proposed that we favor the groups to which we belong in order to enhance our self-esteem.

The **cognitive approach to stereotypes** proposed that the tendency to divide people into social groups is a normal cognitive process. They help us simplify and organize our world. Stereotypes can guide the way we perceive people, make attributions for their behavior, remember them, and evaluate them.

Prejudice can be overcome through education, legislation, and bringing groups into contact with one another to work toward a common goal.

## Problem Solving Examples:

Distinguish between prejudice and discrimination.

Prejudice is an attitude; it is generally a negative attitude held toward a particular group and any member of that group. It is translated into behavior through discrimination. Discrimination is action that results from prejudiced points of view.

It is possible for an individual to be quite prejudiced and still not discriminate. The Equal Rights Laws that have been passed in the past decade have helped to reduce discrimination, but it is less likely that they have reduced covert prejudice as significantly as they have the more obvious forms of discrimination. However, some evidence exists that even the prejudicial attitudes of Americans have been influenced by the laws Congress has passed dealing with ethnic prejudice prohibiting discrimination in voting, employment, and public accommodations. For instance, in 1964, most Americans were opposed to the Civil Rights Act, but today over 75 percent of the public favors integration. In areas in the South where they were previously forbidden to vote, many blacks now hold public office.

In the area of sexism – discrimination based on sex – the woman manager may have won social position and responsibility, but it does not insure that the other men and women she works with will be free of the prejudiced attitudes about women's lack of ability in management (lack of rationality, tendency toward dependence and emotionalism) and other attitudes that may have been acquired and nurtured through many years. When discrimination decreases and prejudice remains, discrimination may begin to take more subtle forms: not being included in the informal discussions of the other managers, being naturally expected to prepare the coffee for the meeting, being assigned the more routine aspects of a particular project, and – an almost impossible variable to measure – being tuned out or listened to through the filter of one or another of the traditional attitudes about women – "she's too emotional," "she needs to be humored until the bad mood passes," "she can't be serious about business," and so forth. These are very subtle forms of discrimination that arise from deeply ingrained prejudiced attitudes.

 What is the difference between a prejudice and a stereotype?

 Although there are both positive and negative prejudices, most research in this area deals with negative prejudice.

Negative prejudice is a negative, hostile attitude toward a specific group of individuals based on incorrect or incomplete knowledge of that group. Stereotyping is the application of generalized characteristics or motives to a group of people, giving the same characteristics to all the people in the group, regardless of the individual characteristics actually present. Stereotyping is not necessarily an intentional act of derogation; very often it is merely used as a means of simplifying the complex world we live in. However, stereotypes can be dangerous when they narrow our views of actual individual differences. Prejudiced attitudes may then result.

## 7.3    Attribution Process

**Attributions** are inferences that people draw about the causes of events, others' behavior, and their own behavior. We make attributions because we want to understand our own behavior, the behavior of others, and the events that take place in our lives. We are most likely to make attributions when:

unusual events grab our attention;

events have personal consequences for us; and

others behave in unexpected ways.

We can classify attributions in a number of ways. One basic distinction is between **internal causes** (a person's personality traits or motives) or **external causes** (environmental or situational factors).

### 7.3.1    Factors Influencing Attributions

**Harold Kelley** proposed three factors that influence whether we make internal (person) attributions or external (situational) attributions:

| | |
|---|---|
| **Consensus** | The degree to which someone's behavior is similar to another's behavior. |
| **Distinctiveness** | Whether the person is responding in a unique way in this situation but would respond differently in other situations. |

**Consistency** — Whether the person responds in the same way on most occasions.

Low consensus + low distinctiveness + high consistency = **Internal** (person) **attribution**.

High consensus + high distinctiveness + high consistency = **External** (situational) **attribution**.

### 7.3.2 Fundamental Attribution Error

The **fundamental attribution error** refers to the tendency to attribute another's behavior to internal (personal) causes (e.g., I attribute my roommate's poor test performance to a lack of ability).

We also tend to overestimate external (situational) causes when explaining our own behavior (e.g., I attribute my poor test performance to an unfair exam). This is sometimes referred to as the **actor-observer bias**. According to the actor-observer bias, we make the fundamental attribution error in judging others, but not when judging ourselves.

We may consider ourselves to be more influenced by situational factors than we do other people because we are more aware of our own situation. This is known as the **information availability hypothesis**.

The **visual perspective hypothesis** argues that we attribute another's behavior to internal causes and our own to external causes because of our visual perspective – we view our surroundings more often than we view ourselves.

Additionally, the more information we know about another person, the more likely we are to consider situational factors when making attributions about them.

Two consequences of attribution errors are that observers are more likely to be wrong than actors when explaining the actor's behavior and observers tend to blame the victim in making judgments.

Another factor affecting attribution error is **self-serving bias**. Self-serving bias is the tendency to attribute behavior that results in a good outcome for us to internal causes and to attribute behavior that results in a bad outcome to external (situational) factors. For example, I attribute doing well on a test to the fact that I am a smart person. I attribute doing poorly on a test to the fact that I had too much other homework (the situation) and could not study sufficiently. I do not attribute poor performance to my (internal) abilities.

## 7.4   Interpersonal Attraction

**Interpersonal attraction** refers to our close relationships with others and those factors that contribute to a relationship being formed.

### 7.4.1   Friendship

Studies of friendships have found three factors that are important in determining who will become friends:

**Similarity**

People are generally attracted to those who are similar to themselves in many ways – similar in age, sex, race, economic status, etc.

**Proximity or Propinquity**

It is easier to develop a friendship with people who are close at hand. Proximity also increases the likelihood of repeated contacts and increased exposure can lead to increased attraction; the **mere exposure effect**. In a classic study at Massachusetts Institute of Technology, **Festinger** found that friends of women who lived in married student housing were most likely to live in the same building. In fact, half of all friends lived on the same floor.

**Attractiveness**

Physical attractiveness is a major factor in attraction for people of all ages. We tend to like attractive people.

## 7.4.2   Love

Overall, the same factors connected with friendships (i.e., similarity, proximity, and attractiveness) are also related to love relationships:

| | |
|---|---|
| **Similarity** | Dating and married couples tend to be similar in age, race, social class, religion, education, intelligence, attitudes, and interests. |
| **Proximity** | We tend to fall in love with people who live nearby. |
| **Attractiveness** | We tend to fall in love with people whose attractiveness matches our own according to the **matching hypothesis**. |

Researchers believe that love is a qualitatively different state than merely liking someone. Love includes physiological arousal, self-disclosure, all-encompassing interest in another individual, fantasizing about the other, and a relatively rapid swing of emotions. Unlike liking, love also includes passion, closeness, fascination, exclusiveness, sexual desire, and intense caring.

Some researchers have distinguished two main types of love:

| | |
|---|---|
| **Passionate or Romantic Love** | Predominates in the early part of a romantic relationship. Includes intense physiological arousal, psychological interest, sexual desire, and the type of love we mean when we say we are "in love" with someone. |
| **Companionate or Affectionate Love** | The type of love that occurs when we have a deep, caring affection for a person. |

**Robert Sternberg** has proposed a **triangular theory of love** that consists of three components:

| | |
|---|---|
| **Intimacy** | The encompassing feelings of closeness and connectedness in a relationship. |

| Passion | The physical and sexual attraction in a relationship. |
|---|---|
| Decision/ Commitment | Encompasses the initial cognition that one loves someone, and the longer-term feelings of commitment to maintain the love. |

According to Sternberg's theory, complete love only happens when all three kinds of love are represented in a relationship. Sternberg called this complete love "**consummate love.**" **Fatuous love** is based on passion and commitment only and is often short-lived.

Research has shown that successful romantic relationships that last for many years are based on the expression of love and admiration, friendship between the partners, a commitment to the relationship, displays of affection, self-disclosure, and offering each other emotional support.

## Problem Solving Examples:

 What effect does propinquity have on interpersonal attraction?

The factor that is found to be most predictive of interpersonal attractiveness is propinquity or degree of physical closeness. The closer two individuals are geographically, the more likely it is that they will like each other. A repeated finding concerning mate selection is that individuals find mates who live close by them. One of the indirect justifications for going away to college is to increase the range of contact with possible partners. If you stop and think of who your best friends are, you will probably realize that you and your friend at one time lived or worked near each other.

One explanation for this finding is that to avoid dissonance between one's attitudes and one's behavior, it would be necessary to like someone with whom one spent a great deal of time. To test this hypothesis, Darley and Berscheid gave women virtually identical descriptions of two people. Then they were told that they would meet and work with one of the two people. Later they were asked to rate how much they liked the two people they had read about. As would be expected from the dissonance theory, the women liked the person they believed they would be meeting and working with significantly more than the person they thought they would never meet.

Another function of propinquity, obviously, is that it makes possible the operation of other factors that can increase attraction such as attitude similarity, which also plays a large role in interpersonal attractiveness. Whether attitudes are actually similar seems less important than whether they are perceived to be similar. Generally, on attitude scales, people rate people they like as having attitudes similar to their own, even if, in fact, this is not true.

 How does reinforcement theory explain friendship? Contrast this with Heider's balance theory.

According to reinforcement theory, the most important factor in whether a friendship will develop and continue is the ratio between the rewards and punishments (or costs) involved in the relationship. Most people prefer relationships that offer more rewards than punishments. Rewards can take the form of attention, praise, love, respect or they can be more tangible such as money, status, good cooking, good conversation. Punishments could take the form of rejection, ridicule, social disapproval, discomfort, being bullied, ignored, nagged or more tangibly, our friend might spend our money and time wastefully.

Another form of positive reinforcement to friendship according to reinforcement theory would be similar attitudes. Reinforcement theorists propose that similar attitudes lead to liking and friendship because it is rewarding to have someone agree with us. And it has been shown experimentally that people react to agreement with their attitudes just as they react to any other positive reinforcer.

Fritz Heider proposed that the key to understanding interpersonal attraction was "balance," a harmonious, non-stress producing state. He also contended that our perception of the attributes of a person controls the way we behave toward him as well as what we expect from him.

The perceptual factors that are most important in Heider's theory are constancy and balance. We will tend to see a person in a set, somewhat unchanging way.

A central function of friendship is to give this constancy to our attitudes about our friend. This constancy produces a certain psychological economy in that it is not necessary for us to change our view of our friend each time we see him or her. It is not necessary that these attitudes that we form about our friend be necessarily true. We perceive him or her as being a certain type of person, generally one with attitudes very similar to our own. The need for a balanced psychological environment explains why we tend to see our friends as people with attitudes similar to our own. People strive to keep their feelings about important issues and important people in their lives in balance or consistent.

## 7.5  Social Pressure

Social pressure from others can influence our behavior.

### 7.5.1  Conformity

**Conformity** occurs when individuals adopt the attitudes or behavior of others because of real or imagined pressure.

**Social norms** are shared standards of behavior. People conform because they are often rewarded for conforming.

The **reciprocity norm** states that people tend to treat others as they have been treated.

Groups of people whom we are like or wish to be like are known as our **reference group**.

The classic studies of conformity were conducted by **Solomon Asch** in the 1950s. Asch demonstrated that college students will often conform with a group, even when the group adopts a position that is clearly incorrect.

Asch asked groups of college students to state which of three comparison lines matched a nearby fourth line and to make their individual responses publicly. Students were tested in groups of six. Five students in each group were hired by the experimenter to give incorrect answers. Asch found that when the first five students made the same choice, though clearly incorrect, the actual participants in the study (i.e., those not hired by the experimenter) conformed by also making this incorrect response on 37% of the trials.

Later studies showed that the tendency to conform is increased when the group is large or a person has low self-esteem. One dissenter (someone who does not conform to the group) decreases the likelihood of conformity. Some studies have found that women are more likely to conform than men.

## Problem Solving Examples:

**Q** If a group of five people are watching a movie and upon conclusion four of them state that the movie was terrible, what will the fifth person (who happened to like the movie) probably say?

**A** To be able to confidently predict the answer to such a question requires some knowledge of the concept of conformity. Although there are numerous factors which go into the decision to conform or not to conform, the fifth person would most likely say that it was a terrible movie. Psychologists basically support two possible reasons for conformity. The first is that the behavior of others might actually convince the conformer that his initial opinion was faulty, or it may be that he wishes to gain some reward or avoid some kind of punishment by conforming. Additional research indicates that seeking reward (i.e., acceptance) or avoiding punishment (i.e., rejection) is more often the case since subjects generally do not conform when able to respond privately. Although nonconformists are idolized by historians and writers, they are not held in such high esteem by those people to whose demands they refuse to conform, supporting beliefs that society prefers conformity to any non-conformity.

**Q** Outline and explain some of the variables that increase or decrease conformity.

**A** One of the factors which is causal in controlling conformity is whether or not the opinion of the majority is unanimous. If the subject is presented with one ally, his probability of conforming to the majority is sharply curtailed. In situations where the confederate "subjects" are unanimous in their judgments, there need not be a large number to elicit conformity from the actual subjects. As few as three other people can elicit conformity from a subject and the amount of this conformity remains consistently the same up to sixteen other people. A method which is frequently used to decrease conformity is having the subject make some form of commitment to his initial judgement. Psychologists testing this have found that conformity with prior commitment drops to about 6% from a 25% conformity rate without prior commitment.

Another factor which is causal in the amount of conformity is the kind of individuals who make up the group. A group which consists of experts, friends of the subject, or people similar to the subject (e.g., other students) is most likely to increase subject conformity.

The final factor which is causal in the amount of conformity exhibited by subjects is the self-esteem of the subjects themselves. As might be expected, individuals with low self-esteem are much more likely to conform in a given situation than individuals with high self-esteem in the same situation.

### 7.5.2  Compliance

**Compliance** occurs when you go along with a request made of you from a person who does not have specific authority over you.

Compliance has been used to encourage people to buy things that they do not need or to do things they do not really want to do. Several different compliance techniques include:

| | |
|---|---|
| **Foot-in-the Door Technique** | A two-step compliance technique in which you first ask a person to agree to a small request and later ask the person to comply with a more important or bigger one. After agreeing to the first, small request, the person has a harder time turning down the second, larger request. |
| **Door-in-the-Face Technique** | A two-step strategy that occurs by first making a request that is so large that it is certain to be denied, and then making a smaller, more reasonable request that is likely to be complied with. |
| **Low-balling** | Getting someone to agree to a commitment first and then adding disagreeable specifics later. |

## Problem Solving Example:

What is conformity? Distinguish between compliance and private acceptance.

The psychological force which causes a person to act in accordance with the expectations of others is called conformity. Conformity can also be a change in behavior or belief toward another person's or group's behavior or belief as a result of real or imagined social pressure. You walk into a classroom and sit down. You notice that the twenty-eight other people in the classroom are all wearing jeans and you are wearing formal clothing. Each time someone looks at you or whispers anything to their neighbor, you are sure they disapprove of your appearance. You become more and more uncomfortable. You become determined to never dress that way again for the class. The next day when you go to class you too are wearing your jeans and feel much more comfortable. This is conformity.

From this example, it should be clear that the pressure may be imaginary. Perhaps the other students were actually admiring your courage in wearing something traditional and different. Regardless of the actual thoughts of the others, your idea that they wanted you to be wearing jeans (real or imagined social pressure), led you to do just that (change your behavior).

This real or imagined pressure can lead to a change in external behavior only or it can lead to a change in private attitude. In the example given above, it is not possible to know if "compliance" – a change only in external behavior – or "private acceptance" – a real attitude change – has occurred. One method of testing to see if private acceptance has taken place is to observe if the behavior is maintained in situations in which the group pressure is lacking. Do you still wear a dress or suit when you go anywhere else other than the class? Do you continue admiring attractive, more dressy clothing and secretly believe that the other students are slobs or lazy or must be drugged by advertising to wear clothes that belong on a ranch? Do you wear your jeans simply to avoid the aggravation of being the focus of their negative judgment? If so, you are complying by wearing your jeans, and your conformity behavior does not reflect a change in your private attitudes.

If, however, you begin to ponder on the advantages of being able to sit wherever and however you want, to run, roll in the grass, climb fences, roller-skate, and so forth, if you are wearing jeans; if you consider the great cost savings you are going to receive by never having to buy anything again but blue jeans and shirts, and the large amount of time you will have once you are liberated from all that shopping to such a point that you don your jeans with a great sigh of relief and set off to class, your conformity behavior is also an indication of a private acceptance of the value of wearing jeans.

Though in this case the distinction between compliance and private acceptance may be clear, it must be realized that in many instances it is difficult, if not impossible, to tell if conformity behavior implies personal attitude change or not. This is particularly true for laboratory experiments attempting to study these two phenomena.

### 7.5.3 Obedience

**Obedience** is a form of compliance that occurs when people follow direct commands, usually from someone in a position of authority.

The classic study of obedience, using "subject-teachers" who were supposed to deliver shocks to "learners," was conducted by **Stanley Milgram**. Milgram found that a large majority of people would obey authority even if obedience caused great pain or was life-threatening to another. Milgram reported that over 85% of his subject-teachers continued to administer what they thought were painful electric shocks of 300 volts to a victim who complained of a heart condition. The vast majority of subjects (greater than 60%) also continued to obey authority and administered what they thought were the maximum, dangerous, severe shocks of 450 volts.

Even though subjects obeyed and delivered the shocks, they displayed considerable distress while doing so. They were observed to sweat, tremble, stutter, bite their lips, and groan, but they continued to administer shocks because they were told the study required them to do so. Actually, no one was shocked though the subjects thought otherwise. Today, the Milgram study would not be considered ethical because of the stress placed on the subjects.

## Problem Solving Example:

**Q** After World War II there was much speculation about the personalities of those who had committed atrocities. What do the findings of Milgram's studies imply about the personalities of Nazi war criminals?

**A** In his studies on the nature of obedience, Stanley Milgram discovered that the average middle-class American male would, under the direction of a legitimate authority figure, administer severe shocks to other individuals in an experimental setting.

Briefly, in his experiments two men were told that they would be taking part in an experiment on the effects of punishment on learning. One man was chosen as the learner (who was actually a confederate in the experiment), the other as the teacher. The learner was taken into an adjoining room and strapped into a chair. The experimenter read the instructions to the learner about a word-list he was to learn, loudly enough so that the teacher-subject could hear. The teacher was placed in front of a generator which could administer shocks from 15 to 450 volts to the learner. Under the shock levels were descriptions of the effects of the shock from "slight shock" to "danger, severe shock." The learning session would begin: the first time the learner would give an incorrect answer, a mild shock was administered, and with each subsequent wrong answer stronger and stronger shocks were administered. Even amidst cries from the learner of "Let me out, I've got a heart condition," the teacher would continue administering the shock, though more and more reluctantly.

Out of the forty males that took part in the initial experiments, twenty-six or 65% went all the way and administered the 450-volt shock. This somewhat alarming finding demonstrated the extent to which ordinary people would comply with the orders of a legitimate authority even to the point of committing cruel and harmful actions on their fellow men.

On a television interview, Milgram stated that he would have no trouble staffing a Nazi-style concentration camp with guards from any middle-sized American town. He based this opinion not on his perception of strong anti-Semitism, but on the evidence his experiments had produced concerning the power of legitimate authorities to evoke obedience to their orders. It is therefore likely that the individuals involved in the atrocities of the German concentration camps were of a personality structure not unlike the average citizen in America today – though uncertain and uncomfortable with the nature of some orders – still willing to carry them out in the name of duty or obedience to a superior or someone vested with legal or social power.

## 7.6　Behavior in Groups

Social psychologists study groups as well as individuals. A **group** consists of two or more individuals who interact and are interdependent.

### 7.6.1　Aggression

**Aggression** is defined as intentionally inflicting physical or psychological harm on others.

About one-third of studies show that males are more aggressive than females, and the differences are larger with children than adults and with physical rather than verbal aggression.

The **frustration-aggression hypothesis** states that frustration produces aggression and that this aggression may be directed at the frustrater or **displaced** onto another target, as in **scapegoating**. However, frustration does not always cause aggression.

According to **social learning theory**, people learn to behave aggressively by observing aggressive models and by having their aggressive responses reinforced. For instance, parents who are belligerent with others or who use physical punishment to discipline their children tend to raise more aggressive offspring.

According to social learning theory, exposure to role models in the mass media, especially television, can influence aggression. Some research demonstrates that adults and children as young as nursery-school age show higher levels of aggression after they view media violence.

## Problem Solving Example:

 What distinctions are made when defining aggression in psychology?

 Because the term is used in so many ways, aggression is very hard to define. Mass murderers and successful salesmen can both be described as being aggressive, but there is obviously a difference between the two.

The defining of aggression in psychology calls for the application of a set of distinctions to aggressive behavior. The first distinction is between harmful versus non-harmful aggression. In this distinction it is the outcome of the behavior which is important. This makes the initial distinction between the killer and the salesman clear. The second distinction concerns the intent of the aggressor. Hitting someone accidentally is not considered aggressive, but hitting someone with the intention of hurting them (even if it doesn't hurt) is. In addition, one final distinction is between aggression which is necessary in the achievement of a goal (as in professional boxing) and aggression which is an end in itself (as in a common street fight).

## 7.6.2 Altruism

**Altruism** or **prosocial behavior** is the selfless concern for the welfare of others that leads to helping behavior.

One of the most widely studied aspects of altruism is **bystander intervention** – whether individuals will intervene and come to the aid of a person in distress. Many years ago, a young woman named **Kitty Genovese** cried out as she was being brutally murdered outside her apartment building in New York City. Thirty-eight neighbors watched and yet no one helped or even called the police. The Kitty Genovese case motivated social psychologists to study why bystanders will or will not intervene and help another individual.

The **bystander effect** states that people are less likely to help someone in an emergency situation when others are present. That is, when several people witness an emergency, each one thinks someone else will help. This appears to be due to **diffusion of responsibility**. Diffusion of responsibility is the tendency for people to feel that the responsibility for helping is shared or diffused among those who are present. The more people that are present in an emergency, therefore, the less personally responsible each individual feels. People tend to think that someone else will help or since no one is helping, possibly the person does not need help.

According to **Latané** and **Darley**, certain steps will occur before a person helps:

- They notice or observe the emergency event.

- They interpret the event as one that requires help.

- They assume responsibility for taking action. (It is here where diffusion of responsibility is likely to take place.)

- After individuals assume responsibility for helping, the decision must next be made concerning what to do.

- They take action and actually help.

Some social psychologists use a **rewards-costs approach** when explaining helping behaviors. The rewards-costs approach states that before a bystander is likely to help, the perceived rewards of helping must outweigh the costs.

Other research has found that individuals who are high in **empathy** – an emotional experience that involves a subjective grasp of another person's feelings – are more likely to help others in need. According to the **empathy-arousal hypothesis**, empathy has the power to motivate altruism.

Other factors that encourage altruism include a realization that help is necessary, being in a good mood, and seeing someone else helping.

Men are more likely to help strangers when an audience is present or when the task is especially dangerous for women. In other situations, however, men and women are equally helpful.

## Problem Solving Example:

 Discuss the relationship between conformity and the "unresponsive" bystander.

**A** Infamous examples of public apathy, such as the murder of Kitty Genovese in the full view of 38 neighbors, caused psychologists to study how impervious to emergencies people have become.

The team of Darley and Latané hypothesized that the number of people witnessing an emergency situation was a causal factor in whether or not anyone tried to help. They hypothesized that this was a direct relationship in that the larger the number of bystanders, the less likely would it be for someone to help. In this respect, non-responding is an act of conformity.

Darley and Latané tested their hypotheses in a number of ways and each time the hypothesis was supported: the more people around, the less likely one of them would help. One plausible explanation given for this effect is that in such a situation, there is a diffusion of responsibility. The bystanders are hypothesized to feel that in a group setting it is not solely their responsibility to aid the victim. Some factors that cause people to help a victim are: a sharing of a "common fate" situation and a situation where there is no escape, no choice but to help.

### 7.6.3 Group Processes

Psychologists also have studied how the presence of a group affects performance and decision making.

**Robert Zajonc** demonstrated that the presence of another person is enough to change one's performance. He proposed that we become aroused and energized when another person is around, and when we are aroused, we are more likely to produce a dominant response.

Zajonc stated that on an easy or well-learned task, the dominant response is the correct response, so we will perform better and faster in the presence of another person. On a difficult task, however, the dominant response is an error, so we will perform worse and more slowly in the presence of another person.

**Social facilitation** is the tendency to do better on easy or well-learned tasks when another person is present.

**Social loafing** is a reduction in effort by individuals when they work in groups as compared to when they work by themselves. A common cause of social loafing is diffusion of responsibility – as group size increases, the responsibility for getting a job done is divided among more people, and many group members ease up because their individual contribution is less recognizable.

When people come together in groups, they often have to make decisions. Social psychologists have found some interesting tendencies in group decision making.

**Risky shift** is the term used to describe the fact that groups often arrive at riskier decisions than individuals do.

**Deindividuation** is the loss of identity as a result of being part of a large group. As a result, social restraints are lessened and impulsive or aggressive tendencies and decisions may dominate.

**Group polarization** occurs when group discussion strengthens a group's dominant point of view and produces a shift toward a more extreme decision. Usually the group's decision is more extreme than its individual members' decisions.

**Groupthink** occurs when members of a cohesive group emphasize agreement or concurrence at the expense of critical thinking. This motivation for harmony and unanimity may result in disastrous decision making. Groupthink has been used to describe the Watergate cover-up, the escalation of the Vietnam War, and why President John F. Kennedy and his advisors could have miscalculated so badly in deciding to invade Cuba at the Bay of Pigs in 1961.

# REA's Test Preps
# The Best in Test Preparation

- REA "Test Preps" are **far more** comprehensive than any other test preparation series
- Each book contains up to **eight** full-length practice tests based on the most recent exams
- **Every** type of question likely to be given on the exams is included
- Answers are accompanied by **full** and **detailed** explanations

*REA has published over 60 Test Preparation volumes in several series. They include:*

**Advanced Placement Exams (APs)**
Biology
Calculus AB & Calculus BC
Chemistry
Computer Science
English Language & Composition
English Literature & Composition
European History
Government & Politics
Physics
Psychology
Statistics
Spanish Language
United States History

**College-Level Examination Program (CLEP)**
Analyzing and Interpreting Literature
College Algebra
Freshman College Composition
General Examinations
General Examinations Review
History of the United States I
Human Growth and Development
Introductory Sociology
Principles of Marketing
Spanish

**SAT II: Subject Tests**
American History
Biology E/M
Chemistry
English Language Proficiency Test
French
German

**SAT II: Subject Tests (cont'd)**
Literature
Mathematics Level IC, IIC
Physics
Spanish
Writing

**Graduate Record Exams (GREs)**
Biology
Chemistry
Computer Science
Economics
Engineering
General
History
Literature in English
Mathematics
Physics
Psychology
Sociology

**ACT** - ACT Assessment

**ASVAB** - Armed Services Vocational Aptitude Battery

**CBEST** - California Basic Educational Skills Test

**CDL** - Commercial Driver License Exam

**CLAST** - College-Level Academic Skills Test

**ELM** - Entry Level Mathematics

**ExCET** - Exam for the Certification of Educators in Texas

**FE (EIT)** - Fundamentals of Engineering Exam

**FE Review** - Fundamentals of Engineering Review

**GED** - High School Equivalency Diploma Exam (U.S. & Canadian editions)

**GMAT** - Graduate Management Admission Test

**LSAT** - Law School Admission Test

**MAT** - Miller Analogies Test

**MCAT** - Medical College Admission Test

**MSAT** - Multiple Subjects Assessment for Teachers

**NJ HSPT**- New Jersey High School Proficiency Test

**PPST** - Pre-Professional Skills Tests

**PRAXIS II/NTE** - Core Battery

**PSAT** - Preliminary Scholastic Assessment Test

**SAT I** - Reasoning Test

**SAT I** - Quick Study & Review

**TASP** - Texas Academic Skills Program

**TOEFL** - Test of English as a Foreign Language

**TOEIC** - Test of English for International Communication

---

**RESEARCH & EDUCATION ASSOCIATION**
61 Ethel Road W. • Piscataway, New Jersey 08854
Phone: (732) 819-8880    **website: www.rea.com**

**Please send me more information about your Test Prep books**

Name _____

Address _____

City _____ State _____ Zip _____